TAROT
FOR
EVERY
DAY

To the Goddess of the sacred
in the everyday

TAROT FOR EVERY DAY

Ideas and Activities for Bringing Tarot Wisdom into Your Daily Life

Cait Johnson

Foreword by Z. Budapest

SHAWANGUNK

The Shawangunk Press, Wappingers Falls, New York

Tarot For Every Day:
*Ideas and Activities for Bringing Tarot Wisdom
into Your Daily Life.*
Copyright © 1994 by Cait Johnson.

Published by The Shawangunk Press
8 Laurel Park, Wappingers Falls, NY 12590.

Text and cover design by Joe Tantillo.
Illustrations copyright © 1994 by Joe Tantillo.

Library of Congress Catalog Card Number 94-67634

ISBN 1-885482-00-0

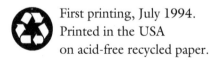 First printing, July 1994.
Printed in the USA
on acid-free recycled paper.

10 9 8 7 6 5 4 3 2 1

CONTENTS

FOREWORD

BY Z. BUDAPEST

The cards in my life were always very important because my mother used them. It was a deck of gypsy cards. She would lay them out and then tell fortunes, but the truth was she simply told stories that came into her head. She actually repeated stories she just heard inside. I never could get anywhere on the gypsy deck. Too many jumps from total sorrow to happiness. What happened in between?

Then came the Tarot. A sophisticated system of seventy-eight, plenty of characters and transitions. I could read cards! Mother was impressed by them also. Today the Tarot is still on the side of the professional. I always advocated that all women should learn at least one good tool of divination to seek counsel when the heart is heavy. The Tarot is the best.

The Tarot's wisdom consoles me. The possibilities that the cards expose to my consciousness are surprising. When I check my progress in life with the Tarot, I am more light-hearted. I feel more assured. My tears dry quicker. My hopes rise higher. I think it's a great blessing.

This book has been written to encourage the use of the Tarot in everyday life. Taking the Tarot away from the sole domain of a Tarot reader, a woman can spend some enjoyable time learning and puzzling out challenges. The meanings are explained clearly; freedom is encouraged to see the truth. It's a great book. Use it.

INTRODUCTION

Many of us have engaged the Tarot in a nourishing partnership that helps us live our lives in the most conscious way possible, consulting the cards regularly for advice, comfort, and guidance. But after we've pulled out our decks, received the images that resonate with our deep selves, and wrapped the cards back up or stuck them back in their little boxes—then what? We can hold those images in our hearts. We can heed the warnings. We can go about our daily lives comforted by the dialogue we have just had with our inner wise one. But what if we could do more?

Even for those of us who consult the cards on a daily basis, the Tarot has always been somewhat set apart from the ordinary fabric of our everyday lives: its occult, mysterious reputation has prevented many of us from seeing what a comforting and down-to-earth helper the cards can be. What if we could bring the Tarot out into our daily lives—manifest its wisdom in concrete, practical ways that will improve and benefit us all? Imagine taking a bath in scented oils that the Tarot helped you to choose, or cooking and eating a special Tarot meal that makes you feel healthier. Imagine allowing the Tarot to suggest colors and clothing that will empower you, or drinking a special cup of Tarot tea to balance your emotions or increase your vitality. These specific, practical applications of traditional Tarot wisdom can unlock a whole new dimension in our experience of the cards and give us an invaluable ally in our journey toward wholeness.

This book offers a way to bridge the gap between the wisdom of the Tarot and everyday life in these very direct and practical ways. It is for all of us who want to live our lives—every aspect of our lives—in conscious alliance with our inner wisdom, working with the Tarot to walk a path of healing and wholeness.

The Tarot can be a much more specific and helpful ally than many of us realize. When used in conjunction with the ancient principle of correspondences, the Tarot can suggest foods, herbs, colors, clothing, and magickal activities to bring us into greater balance. Approached in this practical way, the Tarot joins hands with wise women, kitchen witches, and folk-healers everywhere who rely on the common elements of life to effect their cures, healing the whole person rather than focusing on symptoms, and honoring the ordinary as deeply sacred.

In a world out of balance, it becomes increasingly difficult for us to maintain our own: even if you are free of dis-ease, bringing the inner self into harmony is not an easy task, and the playful Tarot activities suggested in this book can be a great help. Tarot is an expression of the Goddess energy that is beginning to reawaken in the world after centuries of suppression by the dominant patriarchal culture. And the Goddess way offers balance and healing for us as individuals and for the planet as a whole.

The way of the Goddess teaches us to honor ourselves, to reclaim our sacred inner power—the power to heal, to know, to directly experience the numinous. She teaches us to honor the Earth: it becomes our responsibility to stop the destruction of our planet that is her sacred body. And by aligning ourselves with her spirit, which is in everything, we align ourselves with her vast powers of regeneration, both for ourselves and for our beleaguered planet.

By empowering us to find our answers within, Tarot undoes the harm of thousands of years of oppressive, hierarchical thinking that have conditioned us to feel worthless and powerless. If you've been taught to see the world as a dead and meaningless place, then investing the things we touch, eat, and drink with spirit is healing in itself.

Engaging our conscious respect for the small details of our lives—the meals we prepare, the clothing we wear, the substances we put in our baths and on our bodies—gives us a sense of the sacred in the everyday. And these humble, simple things become powerful healing-and-balancing tools when their ingredients are suggested by the Tarot in conjunction with our own inner knowing.

This, then, is a handbook designed with your needs in mind. It is meant to be carried around with you, to be used and explored whenever you need to feel better, wiser, healthier, safer. From special layouts and playful exercises to help you with specific issues, to Tarot recipes and rituals for many different needs and purposes, this book offers a sense of the sacred in the mundane, a nourishing approach to living with wholeness and magickal awareness.

If you are new to Tarot work, you will find that this book gives you a simple and enjoyable opportunity to learn your way around the deck: even if you've never looked at a Tarot card before, you can have immediate access to the wisdom of the cards in order to understand and improve your life. And for those of you who are already friends with Tarot, these quietly revolutionary ideas will start you interacting in exciting new ways with the cards, adding a magickal dimension to your relationship with them.

ONE

Understanding

HOW TAROT WORKS

Tarot's impact is visual and immediate. Its images resonate on a deeper level of our selves than that of ordinary consciousness, the same deep self that speaks to us in dreams. We engage this Deep Self when we do any kind of focused divination, healing, or ritual work. It is a reservoir of healing power, repository of ancient and very specific wisdom, highly individual and yet connected to the universality of human experience. Many of us are only vaguely aware of it. Others are involved in a constant, enlivening dialogue with it. Working with Tarot is one way to become familiar with its infinitely rich and mysterious landscape. The cards teach us about this nighttime, moonlit place: how to find our way around, how to see with what Starhawk calls the "starlight vision."

Tarot also engages the sunlit, rational self. Whenever we consult the Tarot, we are asking for information that is hidden in some way from our conscious mind. But the answers we find in the cards were locked inside us, waiting beneath the surface all along: the cards are simply keys to bring these wise gifts of knowing out of the dark and into the sunlight of conscious comprehension. Tarot teaches us how to live in balance with both worlds.

Approach the cards with an open mind: what they show us about ourselves can sometimes gently deflate our ego, reminding us of old patterns that we have outgrown but cling to out of habit, or of personality flaws that limit our

1

vision of who we can become. But the cards also continually connect us with our best and brightest selves, reminding us always of the most positive path to follow, for our own good and the good of all. And by using the cards as visual reminders of solutions to issues or problems that are of concern, we remain focused on the positive.

Approach the cards with an open heart: the key to establishing a fruitful relationship with them lies in allowing ourselves to become receptive, allowing the images to permeate our inner, deep selves, where transformation and healing take place. Unhappily, though, the reality is that our culture, by honoring only the rational, intellectual modality, has made us pretty impervious: many of us have forgotten or never knew how to unfold to our own sense of mystery and magick. What follows here are some simple, practical methods for stilling our tyrannical head-voices and exploring our ability to open, to become comfortable with our own deeper wisdom.

CREATING A MAGICKAL ATMOSPHERE

Magick—that is, transformative change of consciousness and direct contact with the numinous Power—can happen anywhere, any time. And, although it's not a prerequisite to set the scene in order for magick to occur, if you choose to do so, the likelihood of a magickal experience is certainly greater. In fact, the very creation of a magickal setting not only invites this experience, but it often becomes the experience in and of itself.

So, while advance preparation is not an absolute requirement for the activities in this book—you can go from folding laundry or talking on the phone to doing a Tarot exercise without missing a beat—if you do take just a little extra time, you will add so much to your Tarot experience by giving magick a special place to happen.

There are several ideas offered here for creating a magickal atmosphere around your Tarot work: some take a fair amount of time and thought to achieve, while others are easily accomplished in a minute or less. Take the time you have, knowing that the purpose behind all of the pre-activity suggestions is the same: by creating a sacred feeling around your Tarot work, we tell our inner self to pay attention. We let our Deep Self know that we're ready to listen. We quiet all the trivial nattering that goes on in our heads most of the time so that we can listen. And we reclaim a deep respect for our own inner wisdom.

By taking the time to set the scene for magickal experience, we create something important that will carry over into those aspects of living that we usually think of as ordinary and unimportant: we create a sense of the sacred directly experienced in our lives. Soon it becomes possible for every detail of living to reflect this relationship with the numinous, and we find ourselves living the ordinary life in a most non-ordinary way.

SACRED SPACE

Some of us have already created altars and special places to honor the Goddess and our own spiritual power and connection to her. These sacred spots function as conductors for powerful energy, first drawing us in—they are places where we feel safe and where our spirits are fed by beautiful and special things—and then drawing the energy down to be used for healing or other purposes or to simply be recognized and celebrated.

You can create a magickal space for your Tarot work, making what is, in effect, a temporary altar to honor it. Do this by gathering any or all of the following things and using these elements to create a beautiful place for yourself and the cards.

Special fabric

Silk is traditionally used to wrap the cards and often is spread out to define the area you will be using. If you don't have silk, don't worry—as long as you try to stay away from synthetics, just about any fabric that is pleasing to you will work well. Some of us invest in elaborate batik spreads with moons and stars, or hand-loomed wall-hangings, or antique embroidered shawls. One friend uses a small quilt that she hand-pieced from scraps of old clothes that have personal significance. Another friend uses an inexpensive Indian-print cotton scarf. Whatever works for you is fine.

Candles

For centuries, candles have been used to invoke a sense of the sacred. Natural beeswax tapers with their beautiful honey color and sweet scent remind us of the bees that are special to the Goddess—but inexpensive paraffin candles will do, and if you want to use candles in colors specific for your purposes, they are certainly easier to find in the paraffin variety. Many of us have become fond of the tall novena candles in glass holders that are sold in the Hispanic section of most grocery stores: they come in great colors, including rainbow; they burn for approximately a week; the price is unbelievably low—and they won't catch your house on fire.

Incense

The sense of smell is a direct link with the deep self, as any aromatherapist will tell you. There is an incredible variety of incense on the market today: you could almost choose a different scent for every minute of the day. You can use stick incense or cones or powdered incense, which often includes resins and dried herbs and usually is burned on small charcoal rounds available at religious or occult supply stores. If you've never used charcoal before, you have to try it: get yourself a heat-proof container—earthenware works well, but many ashtrays will do—and fill it partially with sand, earth, ash, or clean kitty litter. Place it on a trivet or a

flat stone. Light one edge of the charcoal round and, when it begins to sparkle, place it in the container. Sitting quietly in the dark as you watch the sparks travel from one edge of the charcoal to the other can completely transfix you—an instant way to achieve the quiet, receptive state so vital to inner work. Some of us prefer to use smudge sticks—bundles of dried herbs, usually sage or cedar, and often including sweetgrass or lavender. Traditional among indigenous Americans, these herbs not only smell wonderful when burned but also clear the space of negativity and give it a clear, pure energy. For those of us who have problems with smoke, an aromatherapy diffuser can give you the scent you want without making you cough: fancy ones are available through catalogues or natural food stores, but you can make a simple one for yourself using a pottery vessel (butter-melting pots are perfect) suspended over a small candle. Fill the pot with water and add the essential oil of your choice. For more information on choosing scents to augment your activity, see chapter 3.

Crystals

Many gem and mineral friends are available to add their beauty to your Tarot work. Some of us use quartz crystals regularly with the cards, placing them on either side of the playing space. You can get quite elaborate here: see chapter 3 for more on crystals and stones. Or you can simply wash a special rock that turned up in your yard and add its grounded solidity to the proceedings.

Sacred images

If you have made or bought a special goddess figurine, this or any other sacred image will be a wonderful ally here, reminding you of your connection with the Deeper Powers.

Nature's gifts

A brown earthenware vase filled with flowers, a perfect winter branch, a spray of berries—all are pleasing reminders of the Earth Mother. Go outdoors and see what calls to you.

Personal mementos

These make a visual statement of who you are, where you're coming from, and what you hold dear: photos of loved ones, symbols of your chosen craft (one artist friend keeps a paintbrush in her vase along with the flowers)— anything that has personal significance to you will work.

It is important to remember that rightness, not elaborateness, is the key here: it can be all too easy to get caught up in finding or buying tons of great stuff that just ends up making your space feel cluttered. Simplicity leaves lots of room for the cards: one or two special things are often enough to create the feeling you want. Here is a cautionary tale: a young friend recently went through a lengthy and elaborate preparation for her Tarot work. Candles were glowing on either side of the perfectly spread silk cloth; dozens of small stones and crystals were placed in precise spiral patterns. She had carefully sprinkled just the right amount of special oil in the simmering pot—and then, just as she was finally ready to start mixing the cards, her toddler woke up. Naptime—and her chance to do any Tarot work that day—was over. Now, when she has a few minutes to herself, she just sits cross-legged on her bed with her favorite chunk of rose quartz next to her, takes a few deep breaths, and dives in.

It is also good to remind yourself that nobody is judging or grading you on your sacred space. It belongs only to you. There are no right or wrong ways to set it up, so don't worry about being correct—if you really want to do your Tarot work on a piece of polyester double-knit, do it! Make a statement. Your final result may be exotic or mysterious or cozy or wacky: what matters is that it feels safe, special, and deeply right to you.

PURIFYING THE SPACE

Once you have gathered your things together and arranged them in a way that feels good to you, you may want to do a salt-and-water blessing and purification for the sacred space you've made. And if you didn't choose to do a formal set-up, performing this simple ritual will help you to feel cleansed of your fears and trivial concerns, ready to focus on your inner work—and will, all by itself, create safe and sacred space.

Use sea salt if you have it, but if not, table salt will do. First put a little salt in a small container that is pleasing to you and put some water in another. This ritual may be performed silently, or you may be inspired to speak.

Hold the salt for a few moments, feeling its earthy energy: it is solid like the earth, which purifies everything that is placed in it. Honor its purifying strength. Now hold the water: feel its movement, the way it changes and shapes itself to any container. Like our tears, water washes things clean. Honor its cleansing strength. Now pour the salt into the water and sense the combination of these two powerful elements. Sprinkle yourself with a few drops of this sacred earth-water. Sprinkle the cards. Sprinkle your space. As you do this, picture yourself and your surroundings becoming cleansed and filled with blessed energy.

If you don't have time for a formal salt-water purification, you can try these simplified versions:

- Put a few drops of sandalwood oil on your fingers and rub your hands together, visualizing that your hands are now cleansed and tingling with positivity.

- Wash your hands in cold water or hold them under cold running water for a few moments: water helps us to wash away and release any unwanted energy.

- Hold a quartz crystal in one or both hands for a few moments and breathe deeply.

- If you don't have quartz crystals, try holding a whole nutmeg in each hand—traditionally, nutmeg was thought to absorb negativity while giving off positivity, like the plants that take in our carbon dioxide and pollutants and exude pure, sweet oxygen. If you don't have any whole nutmeg, sprinkle your hands with salt.

MUGWORT, THE GREEN ALLY

Mugwort is the Tarot herb of choice. Associated with the cards for centuries (as well as with dreams and other divination methods, all connections with the Deep Self), this slightly bitter herb is a natural but powerful relaxant that will help you to let go of tension and align with the slower rhythm of the cards. Steep a generous handful of the dried herb in a teapot filled with boiling water for at least fifteen minutes, strain, and enjoy. If you're short of time, try placing a few drops of mugwort tincture on your tongue before you begin your Tarot session. Once you establish a relationship with wise Mama Mugwort, she will become a true friend whenever you want to deepen. Besides drinking mugwort as a tea or a tincture, you may also burn it on charcoal (like incense) or sprinkle a little on your playing space. Some people store their cards with pinches of it. You can bathe your hands and face in the tea or use it to wipe the dust from your work area or from your crystals and other special objects. The herb itself is a hardy weed that is ridiculously easy to grow: start a mugwort patch and then harvest it lovingly. Chew the fresh leaves instead of gum. Dry bunches of it near your bed. Decorate your space with its graceful stalks or stuff a small pillow with it to help you dream deep dreams. (See chapter 3 for more on dream play with Tarot.) A final word to the wise: although adverse reactions to this herb are rare, it is best to use it, or any other herbal substance, with caution and respect.

PREPARATION RITUALS

As described by Renee Beck and Sydney Barbara Metrick in *The Art of Ritual*, a ritual is "a series of symbolic acts focused toward fulfilling a particular intention." Rituals speak the same language as dreams, as our inner selves, or as the Tarot—here, symbols become the whole expression of the matter. The salt-water and other purification ideas are all preparation rituals: they engage our inner selves and are focused on the intention of cleansing and readying the space. The following short ritual ideas are intended to open the lines of communication with your Deep Self. Try them out and see which ones work for you. Or use these as inspiration to create your own rituals.

• Here is a favorite pre-Tarot ritual: Take a few deep, enlivening breaths. Now rub your hands together briskly and hold them a few inches above the cards, picturing your personal energy flowing from your hands into the deck. Take a deep breath and release it. Now ground the energy by placing your hands, palm down, on the playing space for a few moments.

• Close your eyes and take a few breaths, paying attention to the rhythm of your breathing. Now raise your hands to the sky, inviting the sky-energy to flow down through them and into the cards. Now place your hands, palms down, on the playing space and invite the earth-energy to flow up through them and into the cards. Take a deep breath and open your eyes.

• Sing a short song. Hearing your voice engaged in a rhythmic and repetitive sound will help you to let go of your surface stuff and begin your opening.

• Dip a finger in your purification salt-water and touch it to your eyelids and to the "third eye" in the center of your forehead. Then place a drop in the center of your chest.

• This ritual will look as if you were pulling something out of your heart and dropping it on the cards: place the fingertips of your writing hand in the center of your chest and pull outward. Then open your fingers and spread them, palm down, a few inches above the cards. Repeat this several times.

• Hold the deck to your "third eye" for a few moments with your eyes closed.

- Invoke your favorite goddess, if you have one (see the Suggested Reading section at the end of this book for more information on goddesses).

- Place the cards face down in a pattern. Spirals, circles (with or without an equal-armed cross in the center), triangles, vulval shapes—anything that feels right will work. Look at the pattern you've made for a few moments and then gather the cards together and proceed.

- Hold the deck in one hand and "deal" them face down, one by one, until you have covered the playing space. Then place your hands, palms down, on the cards for a few moments.

- Place the cards, face down, in a circle around you. Close your eyes and picture yourself safe at the center of the circle of Tarot wisdom.

A Word about Basics

The information here is meant for those of you who are just beginning to explore the wonderful world of the cards, but more experienced readers may want to skim this section, too.

Before you can begin to play with this or any other book about Tarot, you need to have a deck that works for you. With the variety of decks available today, you can get a little overwhelmed when you first set out to find one or two that feel especially right. So here are a few guidelines to follow when you find yourself faced with the staggering array of decks at your local bookstore or occult shop.

Take the time to examine as many decks as you can. Ask to see opened display copies so you can really explore the cards. Be sure to get a fully pictorial deck—one with actual scenes for each card, not just a picture of two cups, for example, for the Two of Cups. Sadly, this rules out several beautiful decks, but there are still plenty from which to choose.

In order for a deck to work for you, you have to be able to "see" with it—that is, the images have to speak to you, push you forward, encourage you to make little leaps of consciousness. You don't want to stay trapped in reading the booklet that comes with the deck for your answers: the pictures have to be sufficiently rich and evocative for you to journey with them.

Let your personal aesthetic be your guide: find a deck that appeals to your senses, that looks juicy and beautiful to you. If you have an area of special interest—Native American medicine ways, pagan or Celtic traditions, specific art movements such as Art Nouveau—there are decks with appropriate images that you may want to try.

If you have time, try one or two spreads or activities with the display copy. What do you "see" in the cards? Do the pictures make sense to you? Strike a chord? How do the images relate to your issues? If you are getting information from the cards and the deck is attractive to you, then take it immediately to the check-out counter. (There are some schools of thought that hold that you should never buy yourself a Tarot deck but wait until someone gives you one. Horrors! What if (a) nobody ever does; or, (b) they do, but it's dead wrong for you? There is nothing more frustrating than trying to make a deck work for you that just isn't right. Save yourself the aggravation—decks are highly personal. Invest some time and find a deck or two that will be your friends and partners for life.)

The Rider-Waite and Morgan-Greer decks are two traditional decks that appeal to many people and are widely available, even through mail-order catalogues. Vicki Noble and Karen Vogel's round Motherpeace deck is a brilliant feminist rethinking (or re-feeling) of the Tarot that works well for others. If none of these are right for you, don't give up—enjoy the search!

Once you have a deck, you can begin building a relationship with it. Here is a suggestion that will help you to feel connected to your new deck: After you have looked at every card in the deck one by one, put a pinch of salt and a strand or two of your own hair next to them and wrap the whole thing up in some special fabric that you have chosen to protect the cards. You may want to put a few drops of your favorite essential oil on this protective cloth, so the cards will smell good to you. Sleep with this Tarot bundle under your pillow for an entire lunation (that is, from one full moon to the next). Then unwrap the deck and, by moonlight if possible, do your first Tarot spread or exercise.

If you don't want to wait for an entire month before beginning to work with your deck, don't worry about it— just put it under your pillow at the end of the day.

Now that your deck smells and feels right, you are faced with another challenge: dealing with the frightening or negative cards that are a feature of most decks. Just as life is never unmitigated sweetness and light, neither are Tarot decks, but some of the images can be pretty scary at first glance.

First, the Death card. It is rarely, if ever, an augury of somebody's actual, physical death. Instead, it usually signals a need to let go of something that no longer serves you, something you've outgrown. In the Motherpeace Death card, a snake is shown shedding its skin: this gives us a positive way of viewing this card.

There are several Sword cards in many decks that are violent and painful. These are not indications that somebody is about to attack you with a knife: they are depictions of states of mind. They may not be pleasant states of mind, but recognizing the truth in these pictures of mental anguish is often a first step for healing it.

And then there is the Tower card. People see it and gasp, "Is my house going to burn down? Am I headed for a fatal accident?" The thing to remember here is that, even though the devastation of the Tower looks catastrophic, there is often a figure shown in the card who is calling down the lightning that has caused the Tower to crumble. That figure is you. Your inner self has an uncanny way of knowing what to do to break you out of patterns that are killing you. The more you can surrender to your own knowing, the less catastrophic the event will be.

Here is an example of a Tower-type situation: driving home from work late at night, a stressed-out workaholic accidentally runs off the road and ends up in the hospital for two weeks, where he is able to do nothing but think. He reevaluates the way he is living and later credits the accident with saving his life. But you don't have to become injured or critically ill in order to change things. When the Tower shows up in your Tarot work, ask yourself what part of you is yearning to break loose. Do what you can to free yourself.

Another issue to clarify concerns the reversed cards, which are cards that appear in your work upside down. What to make of them? Some of us do all of our Tarot work with the cards upright. But reversals (or degrees of turning, if you use a round deck) add a lot to the depth of a card's significance for you. Sometimes a reversal completely turns the meaning of the card to its opposite. Other times, it only softens or mitigates it. Let your inner wisdom be your guide. You will often notice that, as you work to clear out the garbage from your life, negative cards that have been appearing in your spreads for weeks suddenly start to show up in the reversed position—and then, when you've finally finished dealing with the issue they represent, they disappear from your work completely.

If you want to learn more about the cards, there are several good books in the Suggested Reading section that will give you some solid basic information; those written by Eden Gray, Rachel Pollack, and Angeles Arrien are all highly recommended. And if you like a more playful approach, try *Tarot Games: 45 Playful Ways to Explore Tarot Cards Together: A New Vision for the Circle of Community,* which I coauthored with Maura D. Shaw: it is filled with enjoyable games for individuals, couples, and groups that help you learn while you play. But remember—you can get real information from the cards even if you know nothing about Tarot by simply seeing the images through your own personal filter.

If you are familiar with traditional approaches to using the Tarot, you will notice immediately that some of the activities suggested here are highly unconventional—but they are never disrespectful. Many of us were taught that we must forever keep our decks wrapped in silk, never let anyone else handle them, never even *show* them to other people. So it can be a bit of a stretch to imagine carrying a special card around with you, or displaying one on a desk or an altar, or playing with the cards in the company of other people. But the Tarot has a power that will survive all this and more—in fact, your relationship with the cards will expand in wonderful ways once you begin to incorporate them into your life. You may want to have one deck that remains wrapped in its silk—and another that you feel comfortable using in all of the many ways described in this book.

When we invite the Tarot, with its rich vocabulary of images and symbols, to become a part of our daily life, we invite our Deep Self and our ordinary consciousness to join hands in a magickal partnership that embraces the totality of who we are. The result is increased appreciation for our own inner wildness and richness and a way of living that is no longer fragmented but whole and vibrantly alive.

As Z. Budapest says in *Grandmother Moon*, "Create culture furiously and diligently by celebrating the Moon and life and yourself. Be the magical glue that creates meaning for our everyday existence. ... Now is the time to claim vision and healing for the next century."

Tarot can show us the way.

Two
Guiding

The most accepted and widely practiced use for the Tarot is as a guide and advisor. Some of us bring out our cards every day for a check-in. Others only do readings on special occasions such as the New Year or our birthdays, or only when we're at a puzzling crossroads, or in crisis. This section is designed to help us get the guidance we need in ways that are easy and enjoyable. But first, the "how to"—because there are ways and ways to ask the cards for guidance.

The best and most helpful approach is to simply ask the Tarot for the information you need. Then you can make wise and informed choices based on this information. The cards, and our own inner wisdom, will actively resist being asked cut-and-dried questions about "what will happen," since the future is affected by the actions you take now. In other words, the future is mutable: you can change the outcome of events based on the decisions you make now. So the cards are there, not to predict, but to put us in touch with the unconscious currents that shape our attitudes, with the unseen forces that affect the present, and with the deep and magickal ability to make wise choices that we all possess.

TAROT SPREADS

I n this section you will find some simple spreads designed to give us loving support and useful information for specific situations, when we need help from the cards and from our inner selves—the times we're most likely to pull out our decks and start asking questions. Use the spreads whenever you need to, knowing that the cards will help you see clearly and act, or choose not to act, from a position of wise knowing and clarity.

YOU AND ME

When you have relationship troubles

Many of us consult the Tarot more about love-related matters than about any other issue. This spread is designed to help you get a grip on the situation in regard to your Significant Other: it can help you sort out your feelings and often shows with surprising clarity what to do about them. You and Me is also a helpful ally when dealing with other types of relationships, such as parental or work-related—any connection with another person that affects you can be better understood through this spread. It operates on the principle that most of who we are is hidden: like an iceberg, only the tip shows on the surface and underneath is a lot of murky stuff that strongly affects a relationship—stuff that we may not be consciously aware of but that we feel. You and Me can help us to understand where our Other is coming from, how we tend to react to her or him, and what we need to know in order to make wise and loving decisions about the relationship.

Mix the cards face down, while holding the image of your Important Person in your mind. Now begin turning over the cards, one by one, making a pile in front of you, until you turn up a court card (King, Queen, Knight, or

Page). This is your Other Person pile. Now once again begin turning over new cards one by one until you reach a second court card. Place it and its preceding cards in another pile in front of you. This is your Me in the Relationship pile. Finally, turn new cards over one by one until you turn up a Major Arcanum. This card, along with the ones that preceded it, is your Right Action pile.

Now, look carefully at your Other Person pile. The court card is a portrait, showing an aspect of the person that is manifesting now, one that may have been hidden from you previously. The other cards in this pile will give you more detailed information about this person: factors in her or his life and personality that make them who they are. If you turned over a court card almost immediately, then hidden factors are not an issue right now; what is clearly manifesting is of primary concern.

Next, examine the Me pile. The court card shows the side of you that most often manifests in the relationship: it is a picture of how you react to your Other. The cards underneath it will tell you why this is so—the buttons that your Other pushes or the factors in your own personality that are important to the relationship.

The Right Action pile gives you vital information about your options that will help you make the clearest decision. Sometimes there are specific things you can do to heal the relationship—and the cards will tell you what these are. Sometimes the best thing to do is leave. But often, we may choose to simply wait and let the relationship unfold, now that we have some perspective on its dynamics. The cards will give you the insight you need as you consider your situation.

Here is an example of this spread in action. Concerned about her marriage of several years, a woman turned up the King of Swords as her Other Person. Agreeing that her husband was manifesting sternness and a judgmental coldness lately, the preceding cards showed her why: the Star reversed pointed to his feelings of not deserving to be happy, while the following three cards—the Devil, Judgment reversed, and the World—gave a picture of someone totally concerned with material, surface reality but unconsciously longing for liberation and expanded consciousness. The Six of Pentacles reversed showed how difficult it was for her husband to receive support of any kind, and showed clearly his current financial worries and feelings that others were taking advantage of him.

Her Me card was the Knight of Rods, showing her present mood of willfulness and need for change—and her passionate search for the spiritual core of life. Beneath this was the Eight of Rods reversed, which showed impatience and her fear of boredom and stagnation. The Nine of Cups reminded her of the emotional stability that her marriage had given her, and the High Priestess showed the role she often played in the marriage: too caught up in business, her husband needed her mysticism and connection with the unseen as a balance for his material focus.

The Right Action pile was topped by the Lovers reversed, preceded by the Queen of Swords reversed and the Ten of Pentacles. The Pentacle card told her how important it was for her to give her husband the sense of family support he needed. The Queen let her know that it was time to let down her defenses, to be more open and less harsh with him. And the Lovers reversed seemed to indicate that, although the relationship was out of balance at the moment, if she could follow through on the advice suggested by the cards, love would eventually flow through them again.

DECISIONS, DECISIONS

When you need to make a choice

When faced with an important decision, some of us make lengthy lists of pros and cons—and then end up deciding on impulse anyway. Some of us talk to our friends for hours and finally realize that we've talked ourselves into a choice. Some of us toss a coin. But all of us can benefit from the kind of information this spread gives us. It is a way to become objective about a situation, taking into account the unseen factors that, not so surprisingly, affect both our choices and our outcomes.

Mix the cards, face down, concentrating on the choices facing you. Then grab a handful of cards for each choice, being clear with yourself about which is which. Now look at each pile, paying particular attention to any Major Arcana that appear. What do the images tell you about each choice? What do you need to consider in each case?

Sometimes we have more options than we think. After you've examined each choice, pick a final card to open your mind to other possibilities. This final card may comment on the choice you need to make for your own good and the good of all.

THE EGG

When you are waiting, or when you feel stuck

If you've been feeling trapped and unable to progress, it may be time to look at the ways in which you have squelched yourself or gotten in your own way. The Egg spread can help us escape from the tight corner into which we've painted ourselves—or, if the factors that imprison us are outside ourselves, the Egg can tell us how to get around them, freeing us to break out of our limited perceptions. You may even find that the Egg you're in is needed for your growth, a necessary time-out as you deepen and mature. Feeling unable to move is one of the most uncomfortable feelings we can have; but this spread reminds us that, even when we feel stuck in waiting, there is activity going on: it's just under the surface. Waiting times can be periods of gestation. However, in our fast-paced society, where the demand is for instant product, immediate gratification, these quiet, dark times are rarely honored. The Egg reminds us of the power that may exist in seeming stillness.

Mix the cards face down and choose seven cards at random. Place them face up in the following pattern:

Card 1 – Where I am now. A picture of my present situation.

Card 2 – Over my head. The roof of the egg. Sometimes an attitude or belief that has put me in the egg, or an overriding feeling.

Cards 3 and 4 – On either side of me. Factors that are shaping my reality at the moment.

Card 5 – Under me. Basis. Foundation. Sometimes shows an issue or event in the past that has put me in the egg.

Card 6 – Hatching out (placed sideways, may be read either upright or reversed). What I need to do or be aware of in order to break out of the egg.

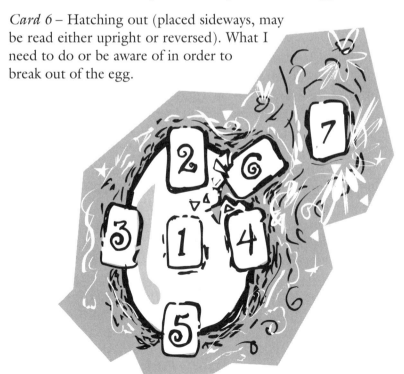

Card 7 – Out of the Egg. How it is likely to be for me once I've broken out of the present situation. Sometimes this card is a clear indication that it's not time to get out yet.

As an example, here is one woman's Egg. Her first card was the Four of Pentacles, which showed her two truths: even though she was fretting about her financial situation, she really had all she needed—but she shouldn't be a spendthrift, either. Her Roof card was the Eight of Pentacles reversed, highlighting her impatience and need to break out of the egg of inactivity that was making her feel low and depressed. Her Either Side cards were the Five of Cups reversed, telling her to focus on the positive rather than dwelling on things that didn't work out, and Strength, reminding her that this egg-time was teaching her how to be balanced and strong. Her Under Me card was the Hermit: she had used this quiet time to listen to her inner Wise One. By stilling outer activity, she made it easier to hear the quiet voice of her inner wisdom. Her Hatching Out card was the Ace of Pentacles, and she realized that a new project she had recently decided to undertake would give her the energy to push her way out of the egg of inactivity. And her Out of the Egg card was the Eight of Pentacles, which showed a person happily working away at a chosen craft.

WITCH'S HAT

Put this on when you need to feel empowered

Good for those days when you feel wimpy or nervous or afraid, Witch's Hat reminds you of the sisterhood of Wise Ones, those free-spirited maidens, radical mamas, and feisty crones who weave a web of strength and wisdom. The shape of a witch's hat reminds us of a cone of power, which begins as a circle and concentrates itself into a point of energy, sent out into the universe like an arrow to the mark. Feel free to cackle as you do this spread.

Mix the cards face down and choose five at random, placing them face up in the following pattern:

Cards 1 and 2 – Wings. The brim of your hat, these cards are placed sideways and read either upright or reversed. They will give you information on what you need in order to take flight, to send your energy out.

Cards 3 and 4 – The Cone. The sides of your hat that lead up to the point, these cards tell you where your power lies or what to do in order to feel strong.

Card 5 – The Point. What you need to send out into the universe, or where you've been aiming. If you don't like the look of this card, examine the others for ways to change it.

For instance, a writer did the Witch's Hat spread because she was feeling unsure of herself. Her Wings were the Ace of Rods and the Sun; both powerful cards of new beginnings and growth, warmth and renewed vitality. She knew this meant that she should concentrate on her creativity, specifically a new book she was about to begin writing, rather than giving in to her lack of confidence. Her Cone cards were the Page of Swords, which she saw as the youthful mental energy she needed in order to do her work, and Judgment, a powerful image of inner liberation: her work would set her free. And her Point card was the Eight of Swords reversed. This was an empowering reversal of a terrible image of being bound and helpless, and it encouraged her, showing her that her work could free others as well as herself.

BROOM

To help you sweep away the garbage

Most of us could use some housecleaning in our lives: old, outgrown attitudes and other mental debris can keep us from realizing our potential. Broom is the spread to try when we need a little help in learning exactly what it is that we need to get rid of and what skills we can call upon to get the job done—an empowering way to make a clean sweep. And it's good to remember that brooms can become magickal vehicles to sweep you up and out of ordinary consciousness.

First, mix the cards face down as you concentrate on doing a little spring-cleaning in your life. Now turn over eight cards and place them in the following pattern:

Cards 1, 2, and 3 – These are placed sideways and read either upright or reversed. They are the dust, the stuff you are working to get rid of.

Cards 4, 5, and 6 – These are the broom bristles, or the ideas you need to apply in order to make your clean sweep. These may identify issues you need to work on before you'll have an effective broom.

Cards 7, 8, and 9 – This is the handle, or what you need to know in order to get a grip on your situation.

NEW MOON

To see how things may grow and develop

Just as we watch the new moon growing from a thin silver thread to a ripe, full circle, this spread gives us a picture of the factors already present in our beginnings that will shape the future. Whenever you want to start something new, think of the New Moon spread and ask the cards to show you how things are likely to develop. Heeding the information in the cards you choose will help you to make things grow and ripen in the most positive way possible.

Mix the cards face down, then choose five cards at random and lay them face up in the New Moon shape:

Card 1 – Began it

Card 2 – Shaped it

Card 3 – At the center of it

Card 4 – Needed by it

Card 5 – Where it is going

Looking carefully at all five cards will give you a picture of the health (or otherwise) of the issue you are contemplating. If you need more information, lay out five more cards, completing the circle.

OUT ON A LIMB

When you're taking a risk

Sometimes we are called upon to take a chance—depart from the safe and accepted path to follow our hearts. At times like these, we may feel as if we are dangling in midair, out on a limb. This spread was designed to give us the support we need and to remind us of the old saying: "When you're out on a limb, you have the world at your feet."

Mix the cards face down. Then choose five cards at random and lay them face up in the following pattern:

Cards 1, 2 and 3 – The tree branch that you're presently out on—the support of the limb in midair. They are placed sideways and read either upright or reversed.

Cards 4 and 5 – The flowering at the end of the branch— that which may occur as a result of your risk. If you don't like the look of these cards, examine them carefully for information. Is this risk worth taking? Is there something else that you can do to make the result more positive?

Recently, a friend decided to take the plunge, quit her job, and start a small business with her partner. Alternately thrilled and terrified, she tried Out on a Limb for guidance. Her branch cards were the Ten of Pentacles (unexpected support from family members in her decision), Temperance (at the center of the limb: learning about her own inner processes leading to harmony in her work relationships), and the King of Pentacles (a comforting image of financial security that reminded her of her partner). Her flowering cards were the Three of Wands and the Four of Wands, wonderful cards that assured her of joy and prosperity.

PENTACLE MAMA

When you have problems with money, job, home or health

Pentacles is the Tarot suit that corresponds with these four areas, so this spread is a sort of handy all-purpose way to get some perspective on any or all of them. And the spread is such a warm, comforting, motherly advisor. Try it when you're feeling ill or down-in-the-dumps, when you're out of work or money is tight, when you're stuck in a job that doesn't satisfy you or when you're looking for a new way to make a living, when your house feels like a war-zone rather than a home, or when you're ready to look for a new place to live. Pentacle Mama will gently tell you what you need to hear in order to improve things.

Mix the cards face down in a pile. While you mix, visualize yourself stirring a nourishing and empowering brew, one that will help you to feel better and see clearly. Then choose five cards (since Pentacles have five points) at random and place them face up in the following pattern: the shape they form recalls sitting in a mother's lap, enfolded and protected by loving arms. Be sure to pay special attention to any Pentacle cards that come up for you, since they will relate strongly to your issues.

Card 1 – You, right now. A picture of what's up with you, what you're feeling, your present situation.

Card 2 – Mama's lap. A stable and secure place to be (placed sideways, may be read either upright or reversed). If the image is negative, look to it for guidance on blocks that need to be removed so that you can find this loving and safe space in your life.

Cards 3 and 4 – Mama's arms. These cards show you what you need in order to feel safe and protected.

Card 5 – Mama's face. Behind the face is a warm, loving, clear-sighted mind that is bending over you, communicating directly to your mind. She gives information you need in order to make things better.

Here is an example of how this spread helped a friend who was worried about her financial situation. She chose the Three of Rods for her first card, which surprised her: evidently, she was in a much better position than she had thought and could serenely wait for the good energy she had sent out to come back to her. Her Lap card, in the second position, was the Four of Swords, which reminded her of her recent recuperation from a lengthy illness that had kept her housebound for weeks. Seeing this as a positive time to rest and recharge, she took the card as a sign that, when it was time to go back out into the world, she would find the energy to do so. Her Arms cards were the Queen of Rods reversed and the Ten of Pentacles. The Pentacle card was important: seeing it enabled her to focus on her need to feel supported by her family in her chosen profession. And the Queen was a reminder that irritability, lack of energy, and depression were results of her illness and needed to be cleared away so that she could more clearly envision a positive future. The final, Face card was the Moon reversed, a sign that she needed to listen to her intuition and not block it as she had been doing, getting caught up instead in pointless worrying. She knew that, when she had managed to get the Moon right-side-up in her life by paying attention to her dreams and listening to her inner voice, the light from her Pentacle Mama's face would shine on her livelihood as brightly as the moon.

REACHING OUT

*When you want to get closer to someone
and you're not sure how*

The image that comes to mind when doing this spread is that of two separate plants sending out tentative shoots or vines toward each other. If both plants do their work, the result will be strong and beautiful foliage.

As you mix the cards face down, visualize the person you want to reach and ask the cards for guidance. Then choose five cards at random and place them face up in a row, in the following order:

Card 1 – The other person. This will give you information about how the person is feeling in relation to you at the moment, or how she or he is appearing to you.

Card 2 – You. How this other person is prompting you to see yourself.

Card 3 – The other person's reaching-out card: what she or he needs to do in order to get closer to you.

Card 4 – Your reaching-out card: the action or attitude you need to take in order to achieve closeness with the other person.

Card 5 – Meeting in the middle: the point of contact.

Negative cards in this spread may mean that you need to examine attitudes or beliefs about yourself or the other person or even be a warning to leave well enough alone at the present time.

EAR OF CORN

To obtain information on the outcome of a project

The shape of this spread is reminiscent of a stalk of wheat or an ear of corn and reminds us of the wisdom of the indigenous people who tended this land. When we are work-

ing to make something "grow corn" for us, it helps to have as much information as possible.

Mix the cards face down. Concentrate on the project, imagining that it has become an ear of corn in your hand, ripe and ready to shuck. As you choose five cards at random and place them face up in the Ear of Corn pattern, visualize that you are peeling away the outer husks to reveal the kernels within. Are the kernels sweet and fresh and firm? Or do you need to rethink some aspect of the planting, tending, or harvesting process?

A friend recently did Ear of Corn for information on a creative project with which she was struggling. She chose the Motherpeace Nine of Discs reversed (taking her healing skills out into the world), the Daughter of Cups (needing to nurture herself and relax), the Four of Swords (taking time out to get herself balanced and together), the Priestess of Wands (channeling her fiery power for the good of all), and the Ace of Swords (using her energy to create). Elated, she saw that her project was important and that she had a contribution to make, but she also promised herself at least an hour of free play time every week, and she signed up the next day for a meditation class. In this way, she managed to take the message of the cards to heart, and she plunged into work on the project with renewed hope and enthusiasm.

Owl

When we want to know what is hidden from us
so that we can take flight

With her age-old reputation for wisdom and vision, Owl becomes our helper when we need to see clearly. Let Owl's eyes see for you, illuminating your life when you feel as if you're in the dark. Then Owl's wings can carry you into the future with the grace that comes from inner knowledge.

Mix the cards face down and then choose seven cards at random, laying them face up in the following pattern:

Cards 1 and 2 – Eyes. These may show you something you didn't see before, which will put matters in a new light.

Card 3 – Beak. Do you need to speak out about something? Or is there something you need to incorporate into your life? Look to this card for sustenance and inner nurturing.

Cards 4, 5, 6, and 7 – Wings. Owl flies silently through the night, brushing our sleeping faces with her soft wings, bringing us dreams. Your magickal wing cards show you what you need in order to soar, giving you information about bringing your dreams into manifestation.

SACRED HAND

***When you want a clear picture
of your own special gifts and powers***

The hand is a uniquely human symbol, evoking images of creativity and the use of hand tools to craft all the artifacts of human society. This spread paints a picture for you of your abilities and gifts, the talents with which you are meant to make your contribution, for the good of all.

Mix the cards face down, then choose five cards at random and lay them face up in the following pattern. If you are left-handed, place card 1 on the far right and lay out the other cards toward the left.

Card 1 – Thumb. What you need to grasp in order to create or produce.

Card 2 – Index. The pointer, showing your focus.

Card 3 – Middle. The longest, most far-reaching of your fingers. An area of greatest strength.

Card 4 – Ring. Thought for centuries to connect with the heart, this finger gives information on your gifts in relation to others.

Card 5 – Pinkie. This may show a possible area of weakness or vulnerability, where you are likely to get caught up.

If your cards are troubled, remember that the hand-shape was used as a healing talisman for centuries. You can use the information given in the cards to heal and transform your life.

Here is an example of the Sacred Hand, for a woman whose life was undergoing radical transformation. Her thumb card was the Motherpeace Daughter of Wands, which showed her rush to embrace the new life and also her need to let go and experience ecstasy. Her index finger was the Hierophant reversed: raised in a restrictive religion, this spir-ited free-thinker took the reversal of this card to mean that the finger was no longer pointing out a "Thou Shalt Not" to her. Her middle finger was the Two of Swords: involved in a hectic and stressful life before her change, she took this as comforting evidence that balance and peace would follow her new choice. Her ring finger was the Seven of Wands, which shows a powerful priestess-figure speaking to a gather-ing. Pleased at this picture of leadership, she felt that her new venture would help her to communicate clearly and from the heart. Her pinkie finger was the Nine of Cups reversed, showing women relaxing around a sacred wishing well dedicated to the Goddess. This told her that she needed to trust her ability to imagine and create a positive future rather than sinking into doubt and fear. And knowing that she had dedicated her own life to the Goddess way further empowered and strengthened her.

TAROT PLAY

There are times when doing a formal spread feels unappealing and we would rather do something simple and playful with the cards, an activity that will still give us the insight we need but will feel a little lighter and easier. This section was designed for those times when our Inner Children are tired of the rigid routine to which we usually subject them and are clamoring to come out and play. Based on the idea that play can be sacred, these activities bring the healing and wisdom of the cards into our lives on a very tangible level. They give us the guidance we need—and they engage our playful child-selves in ways that feel both nourishing and refreshing. And they're a lot of fun.

It almost goes without saying that your children will find these ideas appealing, too—in fact, some of the activities were designed primarily with children in mind. If we can encourage our little ones to look within for their guidance, they will be well on their way to becoming balanced and empowered adults. Tarot cards are naturally fascinating to young people, and these playful ideas enable them to interact directly with the cards in helpful and amusing ways.

And while the concept of Tarot play in community is explored more fully in my earlier book, *Tarot Games: 45 Playful Ways to Explore Tarot Cards Together: A New Vision for the Circle of Community*, you may want to try some of the ideas in this section with a group of your friends. Sharing insights is a wonderful way to become closer and more connected to each other and to your own inner wisdom.

SUIT OF THE DAY

Your current issue, at a glance

Most of our issues and concerns can be divided into four basic categories: physical (finances, job, home, health, the body); mental (intellect, ideas, the rational); spiritual (energy, will, determination, life-force); and emotional (feelings, relationships, intuition). These categories neatly correspond to the four Tarot suits. So, would you like to know what your Issue du Jour is likely to be? Play the Suit of the Day! Simply and powerfully, this little exercise tells us what area is most likely to be our focus. Do it first thing in the morning—or last thing at night, as a way to put the day in perspective.

Mix the cards face down as you silently ask for guidance. Then choose five at random and place them face up in front of you. Count how many of each suit appear. The suit with the most cards is your suit for the day. If you have more Major Arcana than anything else, then powerful and unseen forces are at work in your life: the more clearly you can understand them and work with them, the better your day will be.

Wands	Spirit: energy, will, determination, activity, life-force
Cups	Emotion: feelings, relationships, intuition, creativity
Swords	Intellect: mental powers, ideas, plans, logical thinking
Pentacles	Physical: finances, health, job, home

POWER PERSON

Sometimes our everyday persona needs a boost

This activity is meant for times when we need the added energy or glamour of a court card to help us deal most effectively with our current situation.

Here's how it works: mix the cards face down in a pile. Then turn the cards over one at a time until you find a court card. Look carefully at this card for a moment. How can you bring the energies of this card into your life? How does it counsel you to behave?

An example: A woman who feels financially dependent on her partner turns over the Queen of Pentacles. This card inspires her to feel powerful, as the creator and maintainer of a beautiful, warm home. It also encourages her to think of herself as capable and perfectly able to make a living at whatever profession she chooses. Heartened, she tells her partner that evening that she will find a part-time job.

If you want to bring the energies of your court card even more specifically into your life, try wearing clothes, colors, or jewelry that remind you of or correspond to the energies and image of the card (see chapter 3 for more information). For example, the Queen of Pentacles woman put on a forest-green shirt and a small silver pentacle necklace.

If you don't like the court card you chose, take its message to heart but continue turning cards over until you find one that pleases and inspires you.

POCKET FRIEND

A magickal ally for important times

Suppose you have an important event coming up: a meeting with someone special, a job interview, your first appearance on television—anything that sets this day apart from the ordinary. At a time like this, you want to feel supported and protected. The Tarot can be a wise and strengthening ally, very reassuring and empowering. This little ritual will help you feel ready for anything.

As you mix your cards, face down, silently ask for a friend from the deck who will come along with you to protect and empower you. Then choose a card at random and look at it. If it is a positive one, that will be your pocket friend to help get you through your day.

If the card you choose is not so positive, its message is a warning and gives you information that you need in order to do your best. Heed the warning—and then choose another card at random. Always honor the warnings in the cards but continue choosing until you get a positive one.

Meditate for a moment on the significance of the card you chose. (For example, the Empress would be a fine ally on any creative endeavor. The Queen of Swords reminds you of what a powerful and intelligent person you are and bodes well for matters of communication.)

Place the card in your pocket, backpack, or purse—whatever will keep it close to you. Trace the name and number of the card with your finger over the place where it rests. (For the Empress, you would write "Empress" and "3"; for the Queen of Swords, you would write "Queen" and draw a sword shape.) Making a physical connection with your card friend in this way makes an inner connection as well.

You may wrap the card in cloth, put it in a special pouch, or carry it as is—but be careful: you don't want it to get bent or scratched. There are several small-scale decks available that are perfect for this exercise (the Motherpeace and the Rider-Waite, for example), since they are small enough to be carried anywhere safely and unobtrusively.

By taking the card with you, you will be able to touch it whenever you wish. Or you may simply visualize it, knowing it is safely and secretly tucked away, sending out its powerful message to you. It may "speak" to you at some point— you will hear its voice in your mind, pointing out something you may have overlooked or giving you courage or comfort.

If you want to take the power of your pocket friend a step further, you may choose to wear clothes or jewelry that help embody the energies of the card (see chapter 3 for more information).

Now go on your way, knowing that the energies of the card go with you, ready to give you a big bear hug, an inspiriting pat on the back, or an encouraging wink whenever you need one.

BOX OF BON-BONS

A delicious but non-fattening way to give yourself a treat

We all deserve to feel good about ourselves. Remind yourself what a great person you are by playing Box of Bon-Bons often. Use it as a reward after some accomplishment, or as a way to beat the blues, or just because you feel like it. A way to physicalize your personal affirmation of self-worth, Box of Bon-Bons has serious self-healing behind its silliness.

Play it with friends. Tell each other how wonderful you all are.

First, you will need a box that is large enough to accommodate your cards. If it is special or beautiful, so much the better, but really any old box will do. Now, mix your cards face down while telling yourself that you are wise and powerful, good and talented—whatever adjectives appeal to you at the moment.

Say it out loud if you can. Hearing the words is a good thing.

Now begin turning cards over, one at a time, until you've turned over a total of twenty-one. Read all of them upright—no reversals—and keep every positive card you see. Throw the negative ones aside without paying any attention to them whatsoever. This is one time when you don't want any reminders of your issues or personal flaws. They'll keep. Right now, it's time for a much-needed pat on the back.

After you've turned over your twenty-one cards, pick up the pile of positive cards and look at each of them, long and lovingly. These are your bon-bons, aspects of your self that should make you feel proud. Put the bon-bon cards in your box and place it in a spot where you can see it and be reminded of all of your wonderful attributes. Take down the box from time to time and gloat over the contents. Savor your bon-bons. You deserve a sweet treat.

FROG POND

When you face obstacles

This little exercise looks silly at first glance, but it can be enormously helpful any time you need information on the roadblocks in your path. If you've been clashing with a difficult boss or a quarrelsome family member, or if trees fall on your roof, your cats are breeding superfleas, and your favorite shirt has a hole in it, Frog Pond can make you laugh as it playfully shows you how learning from your troubles can help you to leap ahead.

Mix the cards face down in a pile. This is your frog pond. Now pick a card at random to represent you, the Queen or King Frog. Look at it. What does it tell you about yourself right now? If you don't like the look of it, throw it back in the pond and keep trying until you get a frog card you can live with—but be sure to heed the information that the previous cards gave you. Now turn over up to ten cards at random (ten if things are really rough, fewer if not.) These are your obstacles. Look at them carefully and see how they relate to your present situation. Now arrange them in a pattern that is pleasing to you, spread out on the surface of your frog pond. The obstacle cards are now stepping-stones: make your frog card leap its way from card to card. As it touches each card, the frog is able to change or transmute the card into something more positive: reversed cards may be magickally righted, or worrisome cards may be

reversed and softened. See if there is a healing card for your frog to end up on. If not, know that your frog is at least Queen or King of this particular pond, and use the information provided by the cards to help you calm its troubled waters.

OPEN BOOK

To see your life in clear perspective

This quick and deceptively simple little activity gives you an at-a-glance reality check, illustrations of different aspects of your life that give you the power to see yourself and your current situation objectively.

Mix the cards face down, then gather them back into a neat conventional deck: this is your book. Close your eyes and concentrate on one particular chapter of your life. Now open your "book" at random to see the illustration that goes along with this chapter, issue, or situation. You may repeat this exercise as many times as you wish.

FOOTPRINTS IN THE SNOW

When you feel you've lost your path

Most of us have times when we feel we've somehow taken a wrong turn and gotten off the track that's right for our inner selves. Or we may feel a need for simple confirmation that we are indeed on the path that is right for us. Playing Footprints in the Snow is a gentle way for our wise inner voice to tell us what we need to hear. Feeling that we've lost our way can be a pretty bleak and wintry feeling, but the "footprints" given by the cards become guides that will show us the path.

Mix the cards face down. Now pick up a generous handful of cards at random and stand up. Close your eyes and begin to let the cards fall slowly down, one by one, like snow covering the pathways of your life. When your hands are empty, take a moment to feel how blank and white your world has become. Now open your eyes and look for the cards that have fallen face up. These are your footprints, tracks left in the snow by your wise inner guide for you to see and follow. Look at each of them carefully. Do they make a pattern? Do they seem to relate to each other or lead anywhere? If you can string them together, that's great, but even taken separately the footprints will tell you a story.

WIND

When you wonder what's coming your way

This activity takes very little time but yields a surprising amount of information. Think of it as a fresh, strong wind blowing change into your life.

Mix the cards face down and then gather them into a nice, neat deck. Place the deck face down on the palm of your hand as you visualize the changes that may be about to occur in your life. Now close your eyes and blow, hard, on the pile of cards. Open your eyes and examine those cards that fell from the deck and landed face up. These are pictures of the shifts and changes you may be about to undergo. Cards that fell face down are often the keys to making the changes happen more quickly—or to understanding yourself and your life, so that they can be avoided, if you don't like the look of what's blowing your way. Look to the face-down cards to tell you what action you need to take, or what attitude you need to examine, in order to make your wind a fresh spring breeze rather than a raging whirlwind. Remember that you are in the process of creating your future right now.

WINGED MESSENGERS

When you'd like to communicate with someone far away

Try this activity when you would like to have meaningful

contact with someone at a distance from you (they can be in the next room—actual physical distance is only part of it). Your inner knowing makes the images on the cards speak to you about your feelings and about what the other person is presently experiencing, as well as giving information on your usual modes of communication. The cards, which you send flying through the air like carrier pigeons, will give you valuable insight about the best way to establish contact.

Mix the cards face down and then gather them into the traditional deck or stack. Stand up and take the first ten cards, one by one, from the deck and throw them out into the air. Examine only the cards that land face up. They may be little valentines from your inner self, assuring you that all is well. Or they may point to issues you need to address before heartfelt communication will be possible.

EVENING STAR

To bring peaceful closure to the day

This quiet Tarot activity especially for children is perfect for that twilight time when the fireflies and the evening star have just come out and everyone is thinking about winding down the day. It actually works with people of nearly all ages: children as young as five will enjoy it and find it a gentle way to get ready for sleep (for very young children, you may want to use a deck that doesn't contain any frightening images), and adults will find it a simple, soothing way to put the day in perspective.

Mix the cards, face down, in a pile. You will be choosing three cards at random, one at a time. As you pick up the first card, press it to the center of your chest, saying, "This is in my heart." Then choose a second card, pressing it to your forehead and saying, "This is in my head." Finally, pick up your third card, holding it in your hands and saying, "This will guide and teach me as I make my way to bed." Now look at the cards and see what they tell you. If there are any troublesome issues, this is a perfect opportunity to do some dream-play with Tarot (see chapter 3).

Whenever we allow our conscious minds to relax and let go, inviting our inner voice to speak up with the stimulating help of the cards, we encourage something very precious and magickal to take root in our lives. And by actively seeking the counsel of the Deep Self, we find creative new ways of reacting to our life challenges.

The possibilities for growth and exploration are limitless. And we will have seventy-eight wise and magickal companions and guides on our journey.

THREE
Connecting

This chapter is the heart of *Tarot for Every Day:* the information in its tables and recipes are the keys to exploring and interacting with Tarot in new and magickal ways that you may never have thought possible. And although it may look like a lot of material to assimilate, as with most things that seem complicated at first glance, the seed that sends out such interesting and complex shoots and blossoms is actually very simple. The seed of this chapter, and of much of our interactive work with Tarot, is the principle of correspondences.

CORRESPONDENCES: HUMAN VISIONS OF CONNECTION

Humans have a powerful ability to see the interrelatedness of like things, connecting and categorizing; by placing those like things together in our minds, we create (or discover) a living web that illuminates and ultimately transforms our vision of the world.

For instance, it is a centuries-old tradition that sunflowers correspond to the sun—the small thing, by mimicking certain qualities or possessing similar traits or energies, suggesting something larger. We cannot touch the sun—but we *can* plant a sunflower and invite that warm, round energy into our life. By connecting sun and sunflower, we open a satisfying avenue of action and communication that would otherwise be difficult or impossible. By making this correspondence, we invite a specific representation of a desired energy into our life in tangible form: the sunflower becomes a cue to the Inner Self, a sensory reminder that reinforces the change of consciousness that is often the first prerequisite of other, outward changes. If magick, as the novelist Dion Fortune has said, is "the art of changing consciousness at will," then correspondences are truly magickal helpers; they become our allies in change.

Correspondences can be made between groups of things that seem related or share a dominant quality. The Tarot is already neatly divided into four suits that describe certain life-issues. And just as the four suits of Tarot correspond to those life-issues, they also correspond to the four basic elements that make up our experience of the world.

THE FOUR ELEMENTS
EARTH, WATER, FIRE, AND AIR

*O*ur ancestors knew these four essential elements and honored them as the building blocks of life. Many of us invoke them before we do any kind of magickal work. This is one way for us to order our vision of What Is—by seeing all of life as somehow connected to, related to, or an outgrowth of these embodiments of four very different vital and fundamental energies. By striving to know them wholly, and to express each of them in a deeply conscious way, we find our own sense of balance and wholeness.

The four elements give us a simple way to begin our understanding of life. Being human and finite, we need some way to come to terms with the infinite complexity of our world, of other people, of the human personality. And the four elements lead us on and on: they relate to four basic

personality types, similar to those identified by the great psychoanalyst Carl Jung. And, by simple extension, they relate to certain colors, scents, foods, and herbs.

Here, then, are the four elements, as they correspond to Tarot:

Element	Suit	Direction	Season	Energies
Earth	Pentacles	North	Winter	Material, the physical, form, the tangible
Water	Cups	West	Autumn	Feelings, intuition, emotion
Fire	Wands	South	Summer	Action, passion, drive, will, aggression, spirit
Air	Swords	East	Spring	Intellect, thought, the rational, mental powers

Throughout our lives, we experience each of these great elemental powers to some extent. But we often find that we feel more at home with one or two of them than with the others—we discover that we ourselves are individual embodiments of certain specific energies, just as the sunflower embodies the sun. One ancient and traditional way that people have attempted to understand this phenomenon is through astrology, which, not coincidentally, dovetails quite neatly with the four elements and with the four suits of Tarot.

TAROT AND ASTROLOGY: FINDING YOUR ELEMENT

Astrology is an ancient occult system like the Tarot, and, just as Tarot does, it offers a vocabulary with which we can discuss certain basic ways of behaving in and relating to the world. As long as we continue to recognize and honor the unique complexity of every individual, astrology can give us a valuable way to get a handle on ourselves and the significant others in our lives; our wonderful human ability to categorize becomes a problem only if it leads us into oversimplification, or the pigeonhole trap.

So, one way to begin our interaction with Tarot is to think in astrological terms: how does your astrological information relate to the four Tarot suits? And please remember that your sun sign is just one factor in your chart. For very little cost, you can obtain a complete birth chart with more detailed information that is invaluable when doing any kind of inner work.

Each of the twelve astrological signs corresponds to an element, a personality type, and a Tarot suit.

Sign	Element	Traits	Suit
Aries, Leo, Sagittarius	Fire	Doing: Lively, active, warm, impetuous	Wands
Gemini, Libra, Aquarius	Air	Thinking: Communicative, rational, intellectual	Swords
Cancer, Scorpio,Pisces	Water	Feeling: Emotional, intuitive	Cups
Taurus, Virgo, Capricorn	Earth	Sensing: Grounded, attuned to nature, physical, practical, sensual	Pentacles

Once you have your birth chart, you can quickly figure out your predominant element by counting each sign as one point and adding it all up; most astrologers teach that sun, rising sign, midheaven, and moon are given two points since their influence is felt more strongly. If all of this is new to you and seems unbearably complicated, you may want to look at one or two of the books on astrology in the Suggested Reading section—but it really is easier than it sounds.

Here is an example, using the chart of a friend born in January, under the sign of Capricorn:

Sun in Capricorn = 2 Earth	Mars in Taurus = 1 Earth
Taurus rising = 2 Earth	Jupiter in Scorpio = 1 Water
Capricorn midheaven = 2 Earth	Saturn in Capricorn = 1 Earth
Moon in Pisces = 2 Water	Uranus in Leo = 1 Fire
Mercury in Capricorn = 1 Earth	Neptune in Scorpio = 1 Water
Venus in Aquarius = 1 Air	Pluto in Virgo = 1 Earth

That's a grand total of 10 Earth, 4 Water, 1 Air, 1 Fire. If you want to be even more specific, you can figure out the elemental correspondences for the houses in which the planets are placed, as well. But this simpler view gives a sufficiently clear picture: the person for whom this chart was done is predominantly Pentacle/Earth.

Unfortunately for us Air types, the Sword cards in most traditional decks are pretty hellacious, so if you have Air predominating in your chart, you may want to consult an alternative deck, such as Rachel Pollack's Shining Woman Tarot, with its positive suit of Birds, instead.

Once you know your predominant suit, you can begin consciously celebrating and embodying it. Many of us are familiar with the concept of astrological incense, made with ingredients relating to our sun sign—lighting a stick of it can be a great way to honor your predominant element. But there are many other ways to do this as well, starting with color.

Colors evoke powerful responses. By choosing to wear or surround ourselves with colors that echo our sign/suit/element, we make ourselves more fully at home in our skins and in our environment, and we give ourselves a pleasant reminder that we are in tune with our inner selves. And if there is a marked imbalance in your chart, you can also use this concept to rectify it. (For the Pentacle friend above, wearing fire and air colors might be just the ticket to keep her from feeling stuck in the mud.) In fact, these are two of the basic ways of interacting with Tarot: to honor and celebrate; or to balance and rectify, drawing what you want or need into your life. A third mode of interaction is less personal, involving a desire to know more deeply, to grow in knowledge and understanding of the cards—breathing in the wisdom of the Tarot for its own sake and to learn more about life and the human condition.

Although astrology can help us discover our basic life-suit or element, different phases or experiences will often put us in touch with other elements besides our predominant and most familiar one. The following Tarot exercise can be helpful in identifying the different suit-phases of our lives and helping us to become more conscious about them.

ELEMENTAL LESSON

Mix the cards face down as you concentrate on the suit/element that holds the most important lesson for you right now, at this particular time in your life. Are you in the midst of a fiery Wand time of change or activity? A Cup phase of shifting feelings, strong intuitive knowing, perhaps a longing to merge with another? A Pentacle concentration on material reality—job, home, health—or a feeling of having both feet firmly on the ground? Or a Sword time of testing ideas, puzzling things out, getting your thoughts in order?

When you are ready, choose ten cards at random and place them face up in front of you. Divide them into suits, setting any Major Arcana aside: although these may be examined for relevant information, you will be concentrating on the suit cards for this activity. How do your cards stack up? Are there significantly more of one suit or a fairly even division among them? Are there any suits missing altogether?

Look carefully at your cards, particularly at your predominating suit, if you have one: this is your current elemental lesson. Is there one card that especially appeals to you? If so, you may want to work with color, gemstones, and foods to know it more fully and incorporate it into your life as deeply as possible.

THE COLORS OF TAROT

erhaps the simplest way to begin to embody Tarot energies in your life is through the use of corresponding colors. On a drab morning when your vital energies are low and you want to crawl back into bed rather than face the day, you could make a conscious decision to fire yourself up with Wand colors. Give yourself a little motivation with a burnt-orange hat or a pair of sunny golden socks. Or if your mind has been working overtime and you're feeling on edge, stressed, and ungrounded, you could surround yourself with soothing, nurturing earth colors. Wrap yourself in a warm brown blanket or put on a soft green sweater. Suppose you feel a little misty and emotional today: celebrate your feelings with a scarf dyed in blue-greens and purples. Your color choices reflect who you are and what you want. Wear clothes and decorate your nest in colors that make you feel balanced, serene, and powerful.

The following table gives you some traditional suit/color correspondences, but you can be even more specific in your color work. If you find yourself drawing a certain card over and over, if one of the cards in Elemental Lesson attracts you strongly, or if you have chosen a card to embody a desire or need of yours, bring the colors of that card into your life as closely as you can. For instance, a friend recently became drawn to the Motherpeace Empress card and was so inspired by it that she painted her kitchen the same bright acid-lime green as the background of this card. She also bought herself a leopard-print scarf like the one draped across the Empress figure and began wearing it with pride and a great sense of fun. She reports a feeling of heightened creativity and sensual zest for life.

Wands	Fiery colors: gold, red, orange, deep yellow
Swords	Airy colors: dawn-like pastels, white, pale gray
Cups	Water colors: blues, blue-green, aqua, violet, silver
Pentacles	Earth colors: browns, greens, black

Aside from their Tarot correspondences, colors have other traditional associations, which we perceive in our Deep

Selves. These may be helpful to you if you design your own version of a Tarot card or costume.

White	Innocence, purification, new beginning, serenity
Gray	Protection, invisibility
Black	Power of darkness, earth-womb, night, the occult
Brown	Home, hearth, animals
Purple	Spiritual power, authority
Blue	Protection, spirituality
Green	Fertility, nature magick, prosperity, regeneration
Yellow	Health, happiness, warmth
Orange	Attraction
Pink	Friendship, unconditional love
Red	Passion, sex, aggression, strength, vital energy
Gold	Abundance, success, self-confidence, the sun
Silver	Magick, faeries, the Goddess, the moon

Colors work from the outside in, giving us visual cues that echo in the Deep Self. They can be used in healing ways, as well. On the most basic level, you can surround yourself with warm colors if you have a cold or wear cool blues to help bring down a fever. Many studies linking color with human behavior have shown how vital a presence color is in our lives; when we allow Tarot to suggest the colors of our personal world, we make a connection that both honors and embraces our inner wisdom

GEMSTONES AND TAROT

Traditionally, certain mineral substances have been connected with specific properties, embodying them just as the sun is embodied by the analogous sunflower. Gemstones and other natural substances correspond to Tarot energies: when we partner Tarot with the Earth Mother's gifts, we discover another tangible way to dialogue with the cards.

In choosing specific Tarot-related stones to display, wear, or carry, color is certainly a key, but there are other factors to consider as well. For example, the pastel pink of rose quartz would seem to relate this stone to Air or Swords, but its traditional associations are more Cup-like, corresponding to heart-opening. You may want to consult one of the books on the inner properties of gemstones in the Suggested Reading list; mineral lore can be a fascinating study and an enriching adjunct to our work with the cards.

Use this table of corresponding gems, metals, and other natural substances when choosing jewelry to wear or pieces to display in your home, keeping your own personal energies in mind, as well as your needs and desires. You can find out which stones may be most in synchrony with your inner self right now by doing the Elemental Lesson activity described above.

Wands	Amber, carnelian, citrine, diamond, garnet, gold, ruby, red tourmaline, tigereye, topaz
Swords	Agate, aventurine, feathers, mica, mottled jasper
Cups	Amethyst, aquamarine, azurite, moonstone, mother-of-pearl, pearl, sapphire, seashells, selenium, silver, sodalite
Pentacles	Black tourmaline, copper, emerald, fossils, geodes, granite, green agate, green jasper, jade, hematite, iron, jet, lodestone, malachite, obsidian, onyx, peridot, roots

One colleague has decorated her desk at work with feathers and a big hunk of mica, to help stimulate her intellectual powers. Another woman made a quilt for her bed in rich shades of blue, silver, and violet: she calls it her Dream Quilt and has identified it as a key to unlocking her Cup self. Still another does a periodic ritual where she paints her face with red paint, holds small polished tigereyes in both hands, and invites empowering Wand energies into her life. And many of us choose rings and necklaces to wear in accordance with our sense of our daily needs: amber when we need to feel Wand-like, positive and strong; moonstones and silver for intuitive Cup work; malachite to celebrate the Pentacle Earth Mother. Gemstone jewelry doesn't have to be costly; inexpensive chips and other pieces work just as well to stimulate your inner dialogue with the cards. Check out a gem and mineral show if none of your local shops carry what you're looking for.

The individual cards of the Major Arcana have traditional associations with certain gemstones, as well. You can bring yourself into greater awareness and respect for a specific card simply by holding its corresponding stone and meditating on it: when you open your eyes and heart to the beauty of the stone, you bring yourself into deeper alignment with the card. Place the card upright on your altar or nightstand with the stone at its foot; making this simple visual connection for a few days will greatly strengthen the quality of your card/stone meditation. Then you may choose to wrap the card in special fabric together with the stone to allow their energies to mingle.

Fool	rock crystal, opal	**Strength**	topaz
Magician	tigereye, gold	**Hanged One**	obsidian
High Priestess	pearl, emerald	**Death**	carnelian, lapis lazuli
Empress	rose quartz, coral	**Temperance**	amethyst, garnet
Emperor	ruby	**Devil**	jet, diamond
Hierophant	emerald	**Tower**	jasper, onyx
Lovers	agate	**Star**	fire opal, pearl
Chariot	opal	**Moon**	moonstone
Justice	coral, amber	**Sun**	amber
Hermit	bloodstone, jade	**Judgement**	malachite
Wheel of Fortune	sapphire	**World**	lapis lazuli

Again, your own inner wisdom is always your best guide—if you find a piece of aventurine, for instance, that says "Empress" to you, go ahead and work with it. Feel free to ignore the tables when your inner voice is activated in a contrary direction.

The important thing to remember is how deeply satisfying and exciting it is to discover the many layers of interrelationship in the world. When our smallest choices become imbued with meaning and significance, we become more fully alive.

TAROT COSTUMES: BRINGING THE CARDS TO LIFE WITH CLOTHING

Here is another way to embody the Tarot, almost literally: by choosing fabrics, as well as colors and jewelry, that correspond to the cards to which we are drawn, we can create magickal costumes that make us feel like actual physicalizations of those cards. Imagine what a powerful tool for self-transformation this could be. By becoming the Queen, Priestess, or Shaman, we are making an affirmation for our lives, for our ability to radiate certain qualities in the world.

Your Tarot costumes can be as intricate or as basic as you wish: simplicity and the right feel, not elaboration, are most important. You may want to recreate a specific card as closely as possible (like the friend who draped herself with the Motherpeace Empress's leopard scarf) or come up with your own representations of a helper card, using your original ideas, color correspondences, and the fabric lists given below.

Because life gives few opportunities for a full-blown costume party, you can always adapt your ideas so that they'll be wearable out in the "real world." A full-length Temperance gown would raise a few eyebrows at work or on the street, but you could make a small patch (like the white square with the golden triangle inside shown on the chest of the Rider-Waite Temperance figure) and sew it on a jacket or tote bag. And you can't ordinarily walk around twined with oak leaves and acorns like the Morgan-Greer Queen of Pentacles, but you could do a little subtle embroidery on the collar of a shirt, knowing that every stitch you make is an invocation of her energy.

Wand fabrics	Anything with a golden metallic sheen. Color is really the most important consideration for Wands—just about any fabric will work as long as it's a warm color
Sword fabrics	Chiffon, gauze, batiste; anything thin, sheer, or floaty
Cup fabrics	Iridescent or shiny brocades, satin, silk
Pentacle fabrics	Fake fur, heavy linen or cotton, leather, velvet, wool

Making a piece of Tarot clothing (or finding one, since thrift shops can yield some wonderful costume surprises) and then wearing it with conscious intention to link with a card is a transformative magickal activity. If you want to try it but feel a little overwhelmed or unsure of where to start, you may want to read chapter 5, "Creating," to give you some ideas. Remember that there are no wrong ways to go about this. The cards will tell you what to do: really look at the ones that are seeking you out at the moment. Notice the details, then find a way to put those details on. Deep inside most of us is still the child who loved to play dress-up. Now she can come out, cloaked with magick and power.

MAGICKAL TAROT BATHS AND OTHER DELIGHTS

There is nothing quite so soothing as slipping off daily cares and worries along with our clothes and sinking into a steaming, sweet-scented tub. A magickal bath with essential oils chosen for their correspondences to certain card energies is one of the most powerful gifts we can give ourselves. Both skin and sense of smell are directly connected to our deepest, most primal selves and can do wonders for us if we engage them in a conscious way. Imagine soaking up the magickal psychic powers of the High Priestess as you dream by candlelight, reveling in the earthy sensuality of the Empress, or warming yourself in the glow of the Sun. Try a Queen of Swords bath to make you feel more mentally alert, a Moon bath to help you dream more deeply, or a Queen of Pentacles bath for healing and grounding.

Here, then, is another layer of connection: as well as the table of general card/scent correspondences, there are several recipes for specific baths given. As always, feel free to experiment with the scents that feel right to you. And please be sure to buy real essential oils, not synthetics: our inner selves can really tell the difference, even if our noses can't. You can find essential oils at natural food stores or through mail-order catalogues.

Don't be confused if you see the same scent listed more than once; many of them contain more than one quality or

energy. Sandalwood, for example, appears on all four lists, making it the perfect all-purpose scent.

If you are pregnant, please consult a healthcare professional before using any of these oils; several of them could prove to be harmful.

Wand scents	Allspice, amber, bay, carnation, cinnamon, clove, frankincense, ginger, honeysuckle, lemon, myrrh, orange, sandalwood
Sword scents	Lavender, mint, neroli, rosemary, sandalwood, thyme
Cup scents	Eucalyptus, gardenia, jasmine, lavender, lilac, lotus, rose, musk, sandalwood, violet
Pentacle scents	Cedar, cypress, honeysuckle, patchouli, pine, sandalwood

To get the most from your Magickal Bath experience, it helps to set the stage first: having a relatively clean and tidy bathroom is nice but not absolutely essential. If you can, bathe by candlelight, using candles that are colored or scented appropriately. You may also want to add corresponding gemstones to the water or hold them in your hands as you soak.

Place the card you are invoking where you will see it from your position in the tub, and, as you begin to run the water, think about the card, allowing its image to fill your mind's eye. Then add the essential oils of your choice or according to the recipe, just a few drops at a time, until it smells right. With each addition, imagine that the energies of the card are manifesting more strongly, more deeply.

When your bath is ready, take a deep breath and enter it as you would a mystical experience, a magickal journey. Allow yourself to sink into the water and lie quietly for as long as you like, imagining the powers of the card soaking into your skin, entering your whole self. When you are ready to get out, close your eyes for a moment and take a deep breath. Then, as you stand up, see your skin cloaked with the energies of the card. See yourself becoming the card.

QUEEN OF WANDS BATH

When you need to feel warm, sunny, positive, capable, and strong. This bath is also great for your skin: the honey and olive oil, besides being sun- and Wand-related, are moisturizing. When you get out, your skin will shine!

Several drops each:
    amber, basil, myrrh
A couple of drops of clove (be stingy here—too much
    will burn your skin)
About a quarter cup of honey mixed with a tablespoon
    of olive oil

Stir the tub with a wooden spoon, if you have one, and visualize the bath glowing with golden light. When you step in, inhale the warm aroma and feel yourself filling with Wand power.

QUEEN OF SWORDS BATH

If you want to feel alert and mentally stimulated, try this bath: it will improve your memory, wake you up, and help you think. Perfect for use before exams, interviews—any situation where you need to think fast or remember fully.

Several drops each:
    rosemary, juniper
Add a fresh dill sprig, if you have one, or some dried dill in a muslin bag or cloth, tied with string (the idea is to keep the dill from escaping and your drain clog-free).

As you inhale this refreshing scent, visualize your brain cells tingling and filled with energy.

QUEEN OF CUPS BATH

Delight in dreaminess, indulge yourself, and luxuriate in this sweet and soothing bath. Good for PMS days or times when your feelings need a little nurturing comfort, the Queen of Cups will remind you that life is both sweet and powerful.

Several drops each:
  lavender, lilac, lotus

Fill a muslin bag with plain old dry oats (the same ones you cook for breakfast), tie it shut, get it wet, and use as a washcloth, allowing its wonderful slimy slipperiness to soothe you and nourish your sensitive skin.

QUEEN OF PENTACLES BATH

When you want to feel grounded, stable, and sensual, call on the Queen of Pentacles to help you align yourself with the energies of the green growing things and the healing power of the earth.

Several drops each:
  cedar, patchouli, sandalwood
If you want some additional grounding and healing energy in this bath, add a handful of salt.

As you lie in the bath, picture yourself soaking in a warm forest pool, surrounded by trees and lush greenery. Imagine that rooted, vibrant green energy filling you with its vital power.

HIGH PRIESTESS BATH

This potent bath summons up the intuitive and mystical High Priestess: use it to attune yourself to your inner wisdom and your own psychic power. Celebrate your ability to channel magick.

Several drops each:
  bay, frankincense, sandalwood
A couple of drops of cinnamon (careful—this is another one that can burn you)

As you step into this bath, imagine the scented water swirling around you like a magick cloak. Lie with your eyes closed for as long as you like. Pay special attention to any thoughts or images that come to you.

EMPRESS BATH

Honor your sensuality with this lovely aphrodisiac bath, which also promotes creativity on many levels. (Unless you *want* to conceive a child, be especially careful after this bath!)

Several drops each:
  jasmine, rose, vanilla extract
You may also float a handful of rose petals, fresh or dried, on the water.

This is a perfect bath to share with a partner. If your partner is male, don't worry: Empress energies will not un-man him (just the opposite). But if you wish, you may add a few drops of cedar or pine oil in honor of his maleness.

After your bath, anoint yourself with some jasmine or rose oil and celebrate the tenderness and passion of sensual love with your partner or, if you're solitary, celebrate alone. It's good to know that all acts of love and pleasure are the Goddess's rituals.

STAR BATH

This is a special, spirit-lifting bath, designed to help you feel purified, blessed, and protected after an unpleasant experience or mood has had you in its grip. You may choose to embody the Star image on several of the most popular traditional decks and pour some of the bathwater into the tub from a pitcher. Visualize healing, blessed Star energy streaming into your tub as you pour. If you need extra support right now, invite your closest friends to make this bath for you, pouring in the water, singing to you, and staying with you as you soak. This can be a powerful healing experience.

Several drops each:
> ylang-ylang, lavender, frankincense, sandalwood

Take the time to lie still, allowing the water to wash away any bad feelings and filling your body-spirit with peace and protection. When you are ready to emerge, visualize all pain or unhappiness washing down the drain with the bathwater. You are now cleansed and radiant. Blessed Be.

MOON BATH

To encourage deeper dreams, try this bath before bedtime.

A few drops each:
> cinnamon (careful—too much will burn) and
> peppermint

Add several drops of mugwort tincture or a pot of
    strong mugwort tea

If at all possible after your bath, lie down where the
moon will shine on you for a while. Then go to bed, placing
a pad of paper and pen on your nightstand to record your
dreams when you wake. Sweet dreams!

SUN BATH

Next time you feel depressed or chilled by life, take a
Sun bath to promote health, warmth, joy, and abundance.

Several drops of frankincense
A few drops each (careful, they burn) of cinnamon and
    clove
Peel a lemon or an orange, keeping the peel in one
piece, if possible, and add the peel to your bath. Feel free to
play with it as you soak: try to lift it with your toe or see if
you can sink it with your foot. Rub the peel between your
hands and inhale the luscious aroma.

As you soak and play, imagine all the things you would
like to encourage in your life. What seed-ideas or projects or
dreams would you like to nurture? Visualize the warm water
filling your body-spirit with the power of the Sun to make
things grow. When you step out of the tub, imagine that you
are surrounded with a glowing aura of warmth and energy.

You may want to experiment with combinations that
seem right for other cards. What would a Crone bath be like
for you? Or a Strength bath? Try adding other ingredients to
the recipes already given: one to three cups of milk make a
lovely addition to the Queen of Cups bath, for instance. Or
you could do a completely different version with a few

strands of dried seaweed and some seasalt. Take the time to play, and let your nose be your guide.

What if you don't have a tub or the time for a leisurely bath? Here are some other delightful ways to bring the magick of essential oils into your life:

- make or buy an aromatherapy diffuser (see chapter 1)
- place a few drops on light bulbs before you turn them on
- anoint your cards, either using the "correct" scents for each suit or making up something that smells good to you
- anoint your candles, particularly if you are working to bring certain qualities or energies into your life: burning the oil-anointed candles will help
- dab a drop or two on a handkerchief to carry with you
- place some directly on the skin—but be careful: these are highly concentrated substances and several of them, especially the Wand oils, may burn

You will find that the power of scent will change your mood, your outlook, and your consciousness. Enjoy!

TAROT FOODS: MEALS INSPIRED BY THE CARDS

Have you ever had the feeling that the food you eat doesn't satisfy you completely? That there is an element of nourishment missing from it that has nothing to do with vitamins or minerals? Most of us have discovered that returning a sense of the sacred to the foods we eat is the answer to that awful "I just ate but I still feel hollow" feeling. By becoming conscious about our food—not in the sense of counting calories or grams of fat, but in terms of its inner value and significance—we bring the sacred into everyday life in what is perhaps the most accessible and tangible way possible, three times or so a day.

Many of us have been taught to see cooking as a time-consuming chore that we're better off without. Our culture encourages us to grab it from the freezer and zap it in the microwave, or take it from the box, unwrap it, and pop it in our mouths—and so we have lost our connection to food. This chapter gives us a way to rediscover the magick in the things we eat.

Our ancestors knew all about the magick in food. Every act involving food—hunting and gathering, tilling, planting and harvesting, cooking and eating—was done with a sense of the sacred. In effect, all food-related activities were rituals. And so the food our ancestors ate was filled with the sacred, with spirit value. When we eat, our spirits, as well as our bodies, are crying to be fed.

Those of us who take part in Full Moon gatherings have noticed that what we eat in Circle tastes better and nourishes us more truly than any other food. Meals as simple as lettuce fresh-picked from one woman's garden, a bunch of ripe raspberries from another's brambly hedge, and a round loaf of crusty oat bread just out of the oven, when eaten with that sense of the sacred, become ambrosia fit for a Goddess.

And for those of us who enjoy growing or buying fresh food and preparing it with love and true sensual pleasure, a sacred approach to food gives an even deeper awareness, a rich and meaningful new way to interact, bringing greater fullness and well-being to our lives and the lives of those who eat our meals.

Tarot is our wise and playful partner in choosing the foods and beverages that celebrate our inner selves—that balance and sustain us and give us what we need. With Tarot as our guide, foods become our means to greater health, wholeness, and harmony. Tarot helps us to restore spirit value to the things we eat.

Allow Elemental Lesson to show you where you are, then let your inner wisdom tell you what you need. Recently, an associate identified her present phase as predominantly Swords: immersed in a project that took lots of mental energy, she chose to eat as many Sword foods as she could to help herself get through it. Another colleague, in a not-so-positive Cup phase of weepiness and nightmares, decided that some grounding Pentacle foods, along with soothing Cup foods and more Tarot work to heal her emotional imbalance, would be most helpful to her during that time.

The following table will help you choose what to eat, depending on your inner needs. And, just as with scents, you will notice that foods also resist being treated in a cut-and-dried manner. Consider: oats, like all grains, are traditionally associated with the element of Earth, or Pentacles. But since the grain grows above ground, where it is tossed about by the wind, oats could also be considered an Air, or Sword, food. Then again, oats are soothing to the nerves, balancing the emotions, so they could fall into the Water, or Cups, category. Even the experts often disagree. So here, as with any other intuitive or inner work, your own deep wisdom— your inclinations, your own sense of what is right in each case for you— is your best guide. The information given here is never meant to be followed slavishly but to be used as inspiration, giving you a sense of the possibilities open to you and the choices you can make, for your own good and the good of all.

WAND FOODS

Fiery, spicy foods or foods that blaze with fire's warm colors, as well as flambéed foods, are all related to the Wands suit. They get you moving—literally, sometimes, as well as figuratively—and heat things up, or they remind us of the life-affirming and vivid Sun. Wand foods increase your vital energy.

- barbecued foods—anything cooked over a grill or open fire, as well as Cajun blackened foods and Caribbean jerk sauces

- carrots
- chilis, curries, salsas
- citrus fruits: grapefruits, lemons,oranges, tangerines
- corn and corn products: cornbread, tacos, tortillas
- dandelion flowers
- flaming foods
- garlic, ginger, onions
- jalapenos and other hot chile peppers
- mangoes, pineapples
- marigolds (the flowers are great in salads)
- radishes, tomatoes, red and yellow bell peppers
- sunflower seeds
- Szechuan foods
- yellow, hot, or "strong" spices: bay leaves, cayenne, cinnamon, cloves, coriander, cumin, horseradish, mustard, nutmeg, pepper, saffron, turmeric

Unfortunately, many of us with sensitive systems have difficulty tolerating Wand foods. If you want more Wand energy in your life at mealtimes but spicy food gives you indigestion, try serving a cooler food on a hot-colored plate. Bright yellow, orange, or red round plates are graphically sunny and won't upset your stomach.

SWORD FOODS

These include foods that stimulate the intellect, that are in themselves light and airy, or that correspond to the air-energies of dawn-like new beginnings. There are foods here that you could eat before a big exam, for instance—some of the ingredients promote clear thinking or accurate memory. Or if you've been feeling lethargic and stuck in the mud, these will help pick you up and make you feel clear-headed and inspired.

- artichoke,celery
- caraway, dill, marjoram, oregano, parsley, peppermint, rosemary, sage
- frappéed or whipped light foods, such as angel-food cake
- honey
- lentils

- mulberries
- nuts: almonds, Brazil nuts, chestnuts, hazelnuts, pecans, pine nuts, pistachios, walnuts

- olives
- rice
- smoked foods
- sprouts, such as alfalfa

CUP FOODS

Cup foods are usually pale, cool, and watery, and many of them come from the sea or from fresh water. These generally soothing, mild, and gentle foods encourage us to feel relaxed, peaceful, loving—emotionally balanced and in touch with our feelings. They can also promote psychic sensitivity and deep dreaming.

- avocados
- broccoli, brussels sprouts, cabbage, cauliflower, peas, zucchini
- broths, bouillons, and soups
- coconut
- chilled foods
- cucumber, lettuce
- fish, shellfish, and other seafood
- fruits and berries, such as apples, apricots, blackberries, blueberries, cherries, grapes, nectarines, peaches, pears, plums, raspberries, strawberries

- melons: cantaloupe, casava, honeydew, watermelon
- milk, ice cream, yogurt
- peppermint, vanilla
- sea-vegetables, such as dulse, hijiki, kelp, wakame
- sushi
- tofu

PENTACLE FOODS

To help bring you into loving alignment with your body, these foods gently ground you. Many of them are grown in the earth, or remind you of earth in color or texture, or correspond to the earth-energies of stability and fertility. A lovely antidote to feeling frazzled or "up in the air," Pentacle foods are a comforting and nourishing reminder of Mama Earth.

- apples
- beans
- beets
- butter, cheese
- bread
- eggplants
- grains: barley, oats, rye, wheat
- miso
- mushrooms
- pasta
- paté
- peanuts
- pomegranates
- pumpkins
- root vegetables: carrots, parsnips, potatoes, turnips, rutabagas
- spinach
- thick stews and soups

For those times when you find yourself staring blankly at cupboard or fridge, waiting for a little inspiration, the following Tarot activity may be just what you need to suggest a magickal meal for yourself and the people you love.

MAGICKAL CAULDRON

Mix the cards face down in a pile and stir them with both hands. Visualize stirring a black cast-iron cauldron as you do this, filled with some magickal brew or stew. To see what you could be cooking in your own pot tonight, take a deep breath and ask for guidance. Then choose four cards at random from the pile. Turn them face up and examine them. If you have two or more of a suit, keep these and toss the others back in the pot. (If you don't have any pairs, toss all four back in and try again.) Continue choosing cards at random until you have a total of four cards in one suit. (Major Arcana aren't used for this activity.) This suit will either be the one that you are manifesting strongly at the moment, or it will be one that you may want to invite into your life. Either way, it will make an interesting guide when you put together your next meal. Check out the recipes from the section below and pick one that appeals to you—or you can invent something of your own, using the lists above, your inner wisdom, and your own preferences as your guides.

Consciousness in preparing, as well as choosing, your foods is an essential key. You can make a pleasant ritual out of washing and chopping and stirring, visualizing the positive card energies contained in each ingredient. As the dish takes shape, see the bowl or cooking pot beginning to fill with Tarot goodness. Breathe your prayers for energy, clarity, happiness, and health into the food. Sing while you cook or light a candle in the corresponding color to burn on your countertop as you work.

WAND RECIPES

Hot and Sunny Wand Salad

Wash and chop any or all of the following:

> carrots, cut into thin julienne strips (Wands)
> red and yellow bell peppers
> tomatoes
> radishes
> red onions
> lightly steamed fresh or frozen corn

Mix the ingredients, imagining all the wonderful, warm sun-energy that went into growing these vegetables. Moisten lightly with a Wand dressing made from the following recipe. The salad may be served in cups or on beds of dandelion greens or chicory. Decorate each serving with a small marigold or dandelion flower, if desired.

Wand Dressing

> 1-3 garlic cloves, crushed
> 1 large tomato, seeded, peeled, and chopped
> juice of one lemon
> 2 Tbs. olive oil
> 1/4 tsp. each: cumin, dry mustard, paprika
> dash cayenne

Whisk ingredients together in a small bowl. The dressing may also be used as a marinade for thinly sliced fresh vegetables, such as eggplant, onions, zucchini, tomatoes, or leeks, which then can be grilled, a few minutes on each side, until tender.

Queen of Wands Corn Curry

Sauté in a heavy cooking pot, over medium heat, until tender but not browned:
> 1 Tbs. olive oil
> 1 medium onion, chopped
> 1-3 cloves garlic, crushed

Then add the following:
> 3 cups fresh or frozen corn
> 2 medium tomatoes, chopped
> $1/2$ red bell pepper, chopped
> $1/2$ to 1 cup vegetable broth or stock
> 1 tsp. ground coriander
> $1/2$ tsp. each: salt, ground cumin, turmeric
> 1 poblano pepper, chopped (optional)
> 3 tomatillos, chopped (optional)

Stir with a wooden spoon while you imagine that your pot is radiating Wand energy like a small, round sun. Cover and continue cooking until vegetables are tender but not mushy, stirring occasionally.

Serve hot, with cornbread as an accompaniment. The curry may also be drained and used as a filling for tortilla shells, along with mashed cooked beans or cooked rice, and served with salsa. Makes about 4 servings.

Other ideas for Wand meals include round tamale pie, stuffed red bell peppers, spicy polenta, or grilled veggie kabobs. Fresh pineapple rings or oranges cut into sunny rounds make a fitting dessert for summer Wand meals. If the weather outside is chilly, bake warm gingerbread or spicy cookies.

SWORD RECIPES

As you chop the ingredients for these recipes, imagine that your knife is a sword, cutting away the spots and tough ends and pieces, helping you to shape things into manageable bits. Make the connection between the knife-sword and your mind, which constantly chooses and judges, in the most positive sense.

Wild Sword Salad

This recipe is sure to inspire you.

Mix in a medium salad bowl:

1 cup cooked wild rice

1 cup cooked brown rice

1/2 cup chopped celery

1/2 cup chopped pecans

Whisk in a small bowl:

1 clove garlic, crushed

2 Tbs. olive oil

juice of 1 lemon

salt to taste

Mix all ingredients and serve on a bed of greens. Makes about 4 servings.

Nutty Queen of Swords Lentil Loaf

1 medium onion, chopped

1 Tbs. olive oil

Sauté onion in olive oil over medium heat until translucent but not brown.

Mix with the following ingredients:

2 cups cooked lentils

2 beaten eggs

1/2 cup whole wheat bread crumbs

1/2 cup chopped walnuts

$^1/_2$ tsp. sage
$^1/_2$ cup broth (or more, depending on moistness
  desired)
$^1/_2$ tsp. salt

Place in an oiled loaf pan and bake in a preheated 350° oven for 30 minutes, covered, and an additional 10 minutes, uncovered. Serves 4. With each crunchy bite, picture the food nourishing and stimulating your brain, making you feel clear and light.

Other ideas for Sword dishes include sautéed celery with chopped parsley; rice cooked with walnuts, raisins, and Sword spices; grape leaves stuffed with rice and pistachios; and sprout salad with pine nuts.

For dessert, try this variation of the classic from *Laurel's Kitchen*.

Honey-Almond Cookies

1 cup toasted almond butter
1 cup honey
1 beaten egg
1 $^1/_2$ tsp. almond extract

Cream almond butter and honey together. Stir in egg and almond extract.

Sift together:

$^1/_2$ tsp. salt
$^1/_2$ tsp. baking soda
1 cup whole wheat flour
1 cup unbleached white flour

Stir into almond-honey mixture. Form small walnut-size balls of dough, place on cookie sheet, and press a blanched almond in the center of each one.

Bake in a preheated 350°oven for 10-12 minutes. Makes about 2 dozen cookies.

CUP RECIPES

Here are some foods as smooth and creamy as the Great Mother's milk to quiet your jangled nerves and act as a soothing balm to your emotions.

Cucumber Cup Salad

Peel (if coated with wax) and thinly slice:
1 or 2 cucumbers
Marinate in a mixture of the following:
$\frac{1}{2}$ cup yogurt
2 Tbs. mayonnaise
1 Tbs. lemon juice
a sprinkling of dried dill, if desired
salt to taste
Serve on a bed of lettuce.

Cabbage Fit for the Queen of Cups

Steam 6 cups of fresh cabbage, chopped, with a little water in a large pot until crisp-tender, drain, and set aside. Then make a creamy sauce:

Heat 1 $\frac{1}{2}$ Tbs. olive oil in a medium saucepan, add 2 Tbs. whole wheat flour, and cook for a few minutes to lightly toast the flour. Then add a cup of milk and cook, stirring until thick. If desired, add $\frac{1}{2}$ tsp. dried dill weed.

In a large oiled casserole, layer the steamed cabbage with $\frac{3}{4}$ cup cottage cheese, 1 cup whole wheat bread crumbs, and the creamy sauce. Finish with a topping of crumbs. Bake in a preheated 350° oven for 40 minutes. Serves 4.

Other ideas for Cup dishes include seafood chowders; creamed vegetables or fish; marinated sea-vegetable salads; homemade nori rolls with rice, avocado, and cucumber; and vegetable stir-fry with tofu. If you are making a chowder, broth, or soup, meditate on the Cup-like quality of liquids: they assume the shape of their container. They flow. Think about your own ability to change and flow. As you stir, visualize the soup's ability to cleanse and soothe your feelings and nourish your sensitive spirit.

Then, as a reminder of life's sweet juiciness, try the following recipe for dessert:

Minted Fruit Cup

Wash, pit, and chop any or all of the Cup fruits and melons on the list. Combine them in a medium salad bowl with a sprinkling of fresh lemon juice to prevent discoloration.

Serve in individual Cups, garnished with fresh mint leaves.

You may also serve this with sweetened yogurt. And ice cream or frozen yogurt, as well as chilled fruit pies, make perfect Cup dessert alternatives.

PENTACLE RECIPES

There is nothing quite so warming to the soul as a brown earthenware bowl filled with Pentacle food. It reminds us of the deep, rich darkness of the Earth Mother and of all the delicious roots and other foods she gives us for our nourishment. Heavy and satisfying, Pentacle food helps to ground us, lending something of the Earth's stability to our often scattered and stressful lives.

Prepare these foods slowly and lovingly, savoring each step. As you chop and stir, imagine that roots are growing out of your feet, down through the kitchen floor, down into the Earth. Imagine that you are drawing up Earth energy with every breath you take. Imagine the food filling with sweet, grounded Earth energy.

Beet Queen Salad

Mix the following well-chilled ingredients in a medium salad bowl:

1 cup diced cooked potatoes
1 cup diced cooked beets
$\frac{1}{2}$ cup peas
2 Tbs. fresh parsley, chopped
1 small onion, diced fine

Then moisten with a dressing made of the following:

6 Tbs. yogurt
2 Tbs. mayonnaise
2 Tbs. vinegar
$\frac{1}{2}$ tsp. salt
freshly ground black pepper, to taste

Serve mounded on a brown earthenware plate.

Pentacle Stew

Outside, a cold wind gnaws at the bare trees, but inside the cave of your warm kitchen there is a cauldron of Pentacle Stew bubbling, and you know that the roots reach deep down where no wind blows.

Peel (if desired) and chop into bite-sized cubes any or all of the following:

potatoes
parsnips
carrots
turnips
rutabagas

Sauté the cubed vegetables, along with 1 medium onion, chopped, in 2 Tbs. butter or olive oil for about 10 minutes, until slightly tender and golden.

Add 2 Tbs. whole wheat or unbleached white flour and stir to coat vegetables.

Then stir in 1–2 cups broth or vegetable stock and heat to boiling. Reduce heat and cook, stirring occasionally, for about 40 minutes. Add salt and freshly ground black pepper to taste. Serve hot in earthenware bowls with whole-grain bread as an accompaniment. If you make the bread yourself, try cutting a Pentacle into the dough with a sharp knife before baking.

Other Pentacle menus could include pasta with sautéed eggplant, mushrooms, and gorgonzola cheese; hearty bean soup; baba ghanouj on whole wheat pita rounds; and mushroom-barley casserole.

For dessert, try pumpkin bread or pie; brownies made with peanut butter or carob (chocolate, although it looks earthy, does not have a grounding effect); apple crisp with raisins; or dark and gooey date bars.

A FEW TAROT BEVERAGES

Drinks, especially tea-like infusions of appropriate herbs, are perfect for evoking the energies of a Tarot suit. Here are a few favorite recipes and ideas to get you started.

Hot Wand Toddy

This is the perfect drink to ward off a cold.
Heat in a saucepan:
    1 cup orange juice
    1-3 Tbs. honey
    1-3 Tbs. lemon juice
    1-3 Tbs. brandy or whiskey
    ground clove, cinnamon, and nutmeg to taste
Serve steaming hot in a mug, garnished with a cinnamon stick.

If you have a cold or feel one coming on, here is a broth-based, non-alcoholic friend to warm you up:

Hot Wand Broth for Colds

> To 1 cup hot vegetable broth, add:
> 1 clove garlic, crushed
> $\frac{1}{2}$ tsp. dried thyme
> cayenne to taste
> Drink it as hot as you can stand it.

Sharp as a Sword Tea

For those times when mental keenness is the key, this tea is healthier for you than coffee, and it produces a nice and much less jangled clarity. The taste may have to grow on you, but the effect is good.

Steep the following in 1 cup boiling water for 10 minutes:

> 1 Tbs. each dried peppermint, sage, and rosemary leaves
> Strain and drink, sweetened with honey, if desired.

Cup Smoothie

This creamy treat is a favorite of children and adults alike.

Purée the following in a blender until smooth:

> 1 cup yogurt
> 1 Tbs. honey
> $\frac{1}{2}$-1 cup fruit and berries, any combination from the Cup list
> Serve in a tall glass, garnished with fresh mint.

Soothing Cup

Oatstraw is nourishing and calming to the nerves. The

next time your feelings are on edge, take some advice from the Queen of Cups and relax with a chalice full of this lovely tea.

Steep $\frac{1}{4}$ cup oatstraw in 1 cup boiling water for at least ten minutes. Strain, sweeten with honey if desired, and enjoy.

Dark Pentacle Brews

Coffee and hot chocolate look deceptively Pentacle-like, but their effect is more like a Sword on edge. For a more grounded change of pace, try the hot carob and date- or grain-based coffee substitutes found at your local natural food store—their rich brown color and smooth, sweet earthiness are really satisfying.

Another approach is to stir some blackstrap molasses into a cup of boiling water (nourishing and unusual).

You don't have to stop with the four Tarot suits as inspiration: the Major Arcana, with a little active imagination, can suggest some magickal and exciting meals, as well. Why not invite your friends over for a potluck Crone supper? Or a Star banquet, filled with blessings in food-form? A Moon meal could be entirely white or silver, a Sun meal all yellow, orange, and gold. Strength foods would be nourishing and empowering, and a Lovers meal highly aphrodisiac. You could get together with friends and start a monthly Tarot Feast Club, with different cards as inspiration for wild and magickal meals.

DREAM-PLAY WITH TAROT

Dreams and Tarot speak a similar language, a language of image and symbol that resonates on many levels of the Self at once. Working with dreams, like working with the cards, initiates a magickal dialogue with the inner self. And when we unite our own unique, highly individualized dreams with the deep, dream-images of the Tarot that are shared by all of humanity, we make a most magickal and powerful partnership.

The following activities are designed to help us in several ways; they teach us to feed our dreams with Tarot images. They give us ways to dialogue with our dreams using Tarot's symbol language. And they offer ways to resolve issues brought up in our dreams, with the help of the cards.

Of course, to engage in this Tarot dream-play, you have to be able to remember your dreams. (People often say, "I don't dream!" But they do. We all do. Thousands of people have allowed themselves to sleep while hooked up to electrodes to prove it. But we don't all remember our dreams.) Here are some helpful hints for better dream recall:

- *Make sure you get enough sleep,* or even a little too much. If you're currently on the bare minumim of four or five hours of subsistence sleep a night, you'll be too exhausted to remember much of anything. Most of us have our juiciest dreams after our bodies are rested.
- *Drink a cup of mugwort and rosemary tea before bedtime.* Take a Moon Bath. Sleep on a small pillow stuffed with mugwort. Some crystals are thought to promote dreaming: amethysts are traditional dream-stones, as are opals, bloodstones, and Herkimer diamonds (double-terminated quartz crystals). Some people swear by apophyllite. Do some experimenting and find the stones that appeal to you, then keep them next to your bed or under your pillow.
- *Try to wake yourself in the morning,* rather than allowing an alarm clock to jangle you out of sleep. (To do this, say a repeated affirmation at night right before you go to sleep: "I will wake myself up at 7:00 tomorrow morning." It works. Really.)
- *Keep a pad and pencil next to the bed.* The moment you wake up, write down your dream. Don't put it off: you have

approximately eight minutes before the dream begins to fade. If you wake in the middle of the night after a dream, scribble down the salient points to help you remember the next morning. Try to recall colors, landscapes, people, objects, and the feelings you had in the dream. Be as honest and objective as you can.

- *If you know you had a dream but the details elude you,* try placing your body in the same position as when you had the dream: through some mysterious process, this will often bring back the dream.

- *Keep a dream journal.* Your scribbled notes will be the basis for detailed descriptions of your dreams. Write them in the present tense: it makes the dream more immediate and vivid. ("I am walking along a beach," rather than "I was walking along a beach.") Date your dream entries. Give your dreams titles, using the most important object or action in the dream as inspiration (examples: Shadowy Nuns, Bacchante Sisters, Injured Owl, Touring Russia). Include marginal notes, if you want, describing what was going on in your life at the time that might be relevant to the dream. Reread the journal every few months or so, before bedtime if possible; it will feed your dreams. Look for patterns or repeated images or situations. You may notice that you have the most vivid dreams when you ovulate, or just before or during your moon-time, or when the moon is full. Knowing this, you can prepare for your dreams on those nights.

- *Don't analyze*—dialogue with your dreams. Ask yourself questions: "What does this remind me of? How could this dream relate to my life? What is the dream trying to tell me?" Meditate on your dream images. Free-associate and write down the results. Remember that the more you engage your dreams, the more your inner self will perk up and respond: "She's listening! Great! I'll send her a really powerful dream tonight, then!"

- *Feed your dreams* with lots of strong and magickal imagery to increase your dream vocabulary. The Tarot is a perfect source. So is poetry. So is artwork. Take a look at the paintings of Marc Chagall to see how dreams influenced his work—and allow his work to influence your dreams. Read

something magickal before bed; myths and faery tales are
rooted in the same place as the Tarot and make wonderful
bedtime stories.

- *Do a dream invocation before sleep.* Make up a rhyme or
  poem and repeat it several times. Or do a simple affirmation:
  "Tonight I will dream and I will remember my dreams."

Once you have established a warm relationship with your
dreaming self, you can invite the Tarot to nourish it and to
be your nighttime journey guide and companion. This
bedtime activity will help you to begin.

TAROT BEDTIME SNACK

Get comfortable in bed and place your deck next to you.
Mix the cards with your eyes closed, while you get drowsy.
Then choose a card at random and look carefully at it. Really
notice the details. How does it relate to your life at the
moment? What does it remind you of? Place this card
underneath your pillow. As you drift into sleep, hold the
image of the card gently in your mind. Ask it what it would
like to say to you. Invite it into your dreams.

When you wake, write down what you remember.
Repeat this activity as often as you can until an image or
figure from the card appears in your dreams. This may
happen right away, or it could take a little time. Be patient:
repetition eventually yields powerful results in the dream
world.

After a few days of trying this exercise, one friend
noticed that several Kings, not just the one from the card she
had chosen, began to make guest appearances in her dreams.
She placed King cards around her room, gave them names,
and began asking them questions. She noticed that they have
become progressively more loving and supportive of her.
Another friend has garden images, like the ones in the
Pentacle cards, cropping up in her dreams, which she tends
in her sleep.

When a Tarot image appears in a dream, do what the

King-dreamer did: go to your deck and pick out the cards with those images. Draw them, free-associate with them, or ask them questions. You will often find that the work you do around dreams or that you do while you are actually dreaming (like the woman who gardens in hers) will have powerful repercussions in your life. The friend with the King dreams reports increased self-esteem, while the midnight gardener says she has begun to gestate a powerful creative project.

Our dreams make great advisors; like the cards, they have tapped into a spring of universal wisdom that knows our answers already. We can enlist the help of a card to answer our questions, show us our options, and let us know what is the best path for us to take.

Dream Guide

When you are faced with difficult choices or questions, this activity offers helpful guidance. Like Tarot Bedtime Snack, it may take a few nights to activate, but your persistence will be rewarded.

Based on the nature of your issue, choice, or question, choose a Tarot card to be your Dream Guide. For example, if you are torn between two jobs, the Queen of Pentacles would be a logical choice. Relationship troubles? Ask the Queen of Cups.

Take this card to bed with you and cuddle with it for a few minutes before sleep. In simple terms, tell the figure on the card what is going on with you right now. Ask her to journey into your dreams and come back with answers and advice. Ask a question: "What do I need to know in this situation?" Then place your Guide card under your pillow.

As you drift into sleep, picture the card figure holding your hand and entering your dreams along with you. When you wake, write down your dreams and begin working with them: the answers you receive are often amazingly clear.

RIDING THE NIGHTMARE

All of us have had at least one dream in our lives so terrible that we were afraid to go back to sleep. So we turned on the light, woke up our parents or our partners, reached for a book or turned on the television—anything rather than risk going back into that awful dream. But what if you chose to go back? What if you brought help along this time? What if you went back, armed with the knowledge that no real harm can come to you in a dream anyway, so why not be brave, bold, and adventurous? What if you asked the dream, "What are you trying to tell me?" and went back to find out?

If you are troubled with nightmares or recurring dreams, take heart. The following information and activities will help you to learn and grow from these unpleasant night visitors, so that they will no longer need to plague your sleep.

First, some physiological cause may be the root of your nightmares. Avoid sweets before bedtime; blood sugar imbalances can trigger a nightmare. Drugs and alcohol are also likely to cause them. Stress is another factor. Try taking a soothing bath, gently massaging your feet, or meditating for a few minutes before going to bed.

But if there doesn't seem to be a physical reason for your nightmares, remember—there are no "bad" dreams. If your inner self is trying to tell you something and you're not listening, it may have to shout to wake you up. The thing to do is to try to uncover the significance of the dream—pay attention, get the message, so that your inner self is satisfied that you heard. The following activity can help.

Choose a card that summons up your nightmare or your feelings about it; the Nine of Swords in most decks is a graphic representation of nightmares in general, or you could find another card whose image evokes your own.

Then find your Dream Guide card and ask for its help: when you are new to this kind of work, it's good to know that you're not alone. Tell your Guide card about your dream. Describe it in as much detail as possible. If you have written it down in your dream journal, read the entry aloud to your Guide and show her your nightmare card.

When you are ready for bed, ask your Guide to help you unravel the meaning of the dream. Ask for information. Put both cards under your pillow. In the morning, write down what you remember. Free-association will be a helpful approach with this. Allow your mind to wander. Write down everything that comes to you. The images and connections that occur to you will be your keys to understanding.

Soon you may be ready to try going back into the dream. This may be done in the form of a creative visualization, or you may invoke the nightmare right before sleep and dream your way back. Remind yourself before sleep that you have magickal help now and that you bring with you everything you need to understand the dream. Put your Guide card under your pillow and tell her you're ready to try going back. Visualize yourself like the Rider-Waite Sun card, riding the nightmare joyously, fearlessly. In the morning, write down what you remember.

With the help of Tarot, many of us have actually dreamed different, self-affirming endings to our recurring nightmares. And the real irony is that, once you become practiced at dealing with nightmares in this way and are no longer afraid of them—when, in fact, you start looking forward to them as exciting challenges—you usually stop having them completely.

VISUALIZATION: ENTERING THE WORLD OF TAROT

There is a simple technique, easy to learn and enjoyable to practice, that makes our final and perhaps most important connection with Tarot. The technique is called visualization, and it allows you to enter the world of Tarot, giving you access to all of the enthralling scents and sights and sounds of the cards, allowing you to wander in the court of Queens, talk with Priestesses of healing and follow animals to mystical landscapes where you will be filled with wonder. Using visualization, we make a connection to the cards with all five senses, and we contact a level of consciousness that often feels more real than real. It brings our experience of the cards home to the Deep Self in a direct and powerful way.

If you have never done a visualization before, don't worry—even though many beginners' first response to the idea is "I can't do that!" you can. Visualization sounds mysterious and difficult, but if you see pictures in your mind when you read a book, you're doing it already. Humans visualize: it seems to be one of our gifts. If you want more background information, read Diane Mariechild's *Mother Wit: A Guide to Healing and Psychic Development*, Shakti Gawain's *Creative Visualization,* or Starhawk's chapter on visualization in her marvelous *The Spiral Dance.*

You can begin your magickal visualization journey immediately. Just keep these three steps in mind.

1. *Relax.* Sit comfortably with your eyes closed and simply pay attention to your breathing. Don't try to speed it up or slow it down: just notice how it ebbs and flows. Allow your muscles to relax, starting with your feet and working your way up. You may find that soothing music will help you to deepen. Scent is also helpful: try different incenses or essential oil blends in your aromatherapy pot. Feel your body growing heavy and soft.

2. *Ground.* Grounding simply means allowing the energy of the earth to flow through you, so that your own vital reserves are not depleted. Picture little white roots growing out of your sit-bones, growing down through the floor, down into the earth. Picture the roots drawing up the life-giving energy of the earth, the energy that nourishes and

sustains all life. Feel your body filling with earth-energy. Then allow the energy to burst from the top of your head in beautiful branches, branches that arch back down to the earth again. Picture yourself sitting in the center of a magickal circle of energy.

3. *Protect yourself.* Whenever you do inner work of any kind, it is helpful to create a sense of safe space. You can do this by imagining that you are surrounded by a glowing bubble of light, or that you are safe in the Mother's arms. If you like, you may prepare your space beforehand with salt-water or smudge: the lingering scent is also relaxing and grounding. Remind yourself that you are safe and protected, that you can return to ordinary waking reality at any time, and that you will remember everything you experience.

Now you're ready to journey within. Practice with the following exercise.

CUP VISUALIZATION

Picture yourself standing at a table. On the table is a large Cup. What does it look like? Picture yourself picking it up and turning it lovingly in your hands. What does it seem to be made of? How does it feel? Is it heavy? Is it warm to your touch or cool? How is it decorated?

Take a few moments to explore the outside of your Cup. Then, when you are ready, look inside. What do you see? If there is a liquid in your Cup, taste it. How does it taste? What does it remind you of? Inhale its scent with pleasure.

When you are ready, put the Cup back on the table. Take a deep breath and open your eyes.

With just a little practice, you will become comfortable and familiar with the wonderful technique of visualization, which is such an enriching adjunct to our experience of the cards. You will find it to be especially helpful in the next chapter.

FOUR
Healing

our yourself a cup of soothing tea and get comfortable. This chapter is a loving, nurturing approach
to healing yourself and feeling better with Tarot in
partnership with Wise Woman ways. You will find some new
techniques for working with the cards here, ways to help us
access our own healing power and feel good about ourselves.
But to understand how the Tarot can help us to heal, first we
need to look at the nature of dis-ease.

Illness is often a sign that something has reached a pitch
that can no longer be denied; if we haven't acknowledged
the problem area or taken steps to change things—if we have
ignored our inner selves—our bodies will give us a clear picture of what needs to be addressed. Continual suppression of
stress, anger, or grief leads to imbalance and dis-ease. No
longer at ease or comfortable in our bodies, we can begin
the true healing from within by looking at the issues that
threw us off-center in the first place; with forgiveness and
loving self-awareness, we begin to understand and heal ourselves—and Tarot offers a gentle way to open into greater
self-understanding. But this does not mean to imply that if
we get sick, we weren't self-aware enough—or that if we are
sufficiently self-aware, we'll never get sick.

Illness is an inescapable part of living—but rather than
seeing it as a burden or a curse, we can choose to honor illness as one of our most insightful allies and teachers. As
Susun Weed says in her brilliant *Healing Wise,* "Pain is
unavoidable, but suffering is optional." By giving ourselves

94

unconditional love, compassion, and nourishment when we "fall ill," we rethink our vision of sickness and heal ourselves from the spirit-wounds that our culture has given us around issues of health.

All too many of us get stuck in self-blame when we get sick: "It's my fault. I did something wrong. I'm a bad person. I wasn't pure enough, conscious enough. I ate a candy-bar yesterday. I need to fast, do penance, have a colonic to cleanse my nasty, polluted system." This mindset is not only guilt-giving—it also not so subtly reinforces the idea that our physical selves are lowly and inferior to the pure light of spirit, rather than honoring our bodies for the wise and powerful miracles they are. Then there is the other common attitude: "*I* don't know what's wrong with me. I'd better go see a doctor. The doctor will know what to do. Then I can take some pills to fix it. Poor me." This mindset takes away our sense of personal power and hands it over to the established medical professionals, with their emphasis on treating symptoms rather than the whole person. And it disconnects us from our inner selves: the body becomes a kind of machine with a part out of order that needs fixing.

Happily, there is another option when dealing with illness or injury. As Susun Weed points out, there is a Wise Woman way that makes a teacher and ally of illness and heals by nourishing. We can put ourselves back together in wholeness and learn much from our dis-ease by asking questions such as, "What does this illness have to teach me? What is it trying to show me? How is it my ally?"

There are times when our illness simply may have been brought on by contact with a nasty bug on a day when fatigue, stress, or a bad mood had our immune systems depressed. We don't have any big issues to wrestle with here, other than a need to take kinder care of ourselves—we just want to get better as quickly as possible. Or our illness may be the result of tension or emotional suppression, which has become focused in a specific area of the body. In either case, what we need is less self-blame and more nourishing self-care: eating and drinking wild, unprocessed foods and juices are healing. Laughter or a cleansing burst of anger can be healing. And we need nourishment for our inner selves—because true wholeness and health are not brought about by simply palliating symptoms but by listening to and lovingly nurturing the *whole* self.

So how can Tarot help? In two ways, and on two different levels: (1) by helping us to see underlying causes and suggesting practical ways to resolve them, the Tarot works with the conscious mind to effect loving, healthy self-awareness and necessary change; and (2) Tarot nourishes the Deep Self by presenting powerful images that speak to the heart of the matter and work real, healing magick from deep within.

For example, if recurring bladder infections are part of your life, forgive yourself and reach for lots of water, cranberry juice, and nourishing burdock seed tea, by all means—but also ask yourself what is literally pissing you off. The Tarot can show you a picture of the problem and suggest ways to help. Then feed your inner self with Tarot images of peaceful serenity, or empowering release of anger, to begin the healing from inside.

By refusing to see ourselves as helpless victims—by knowing that, with good counsel and guidance from our inner selves, we can work to change the things that wound and damage us, nourishing and loving ourselves all the while—we bring hope and wholeness into our lives.

Do use the sense the Goddess gave you: if you have a bleeding ulcer and the cards are always coming up Wands, don't dust your food with cayenne—look for the suppressed anger that may be eating you up inside. And while we're on the subject of anger, it is good to remember that our most important healing work is not a matter of fixing but of honoring. Honor your fire—don't necessarily try to quench it or cool off.

You don't actually have to be ill or in pain to do these activities, either; many of the exercises will give you satisfying and helpful information that can prevent you from getting sick. Why wait? Many of us have discovered that listening to our inner selves is a form of self-nourishment that gives a great boost to the immune system.

TAROT HEALING EXERCISES

*S*everal of the exercises here combine Tarot imagery and creative visualization; if you are unfamiliar with this simple technique, you will want to reread that section in chapter 3.

You may want to start a healing book: many of us have found that keeping a record of the Tarot work we do around our healing issues, as well as listings of natural remedies and nourishing foods and their effects, is a powerful tool for self-healing.

And please remember that none of this work with Tarot should take the place of responsible self-care or of treatment by a health professional when needed.

YOUR SACRED BODY

How can we love ourselves unconditionally when we are continually bombarded with negative messages about our bodies? Every day we're up against an entire campaign that makes women, especially, see themselves as not thin enough, not beautiful enough, not good enough. Many of us are suffering needlessly from massive insecurity about our physical selves. There are women out there who are starving themselves to death in the name of some impossible ideal of "perfection." (The perfect woman is so thin that she is powerless? Or the perfect woman is a dead but decorative woman?)

Madison Avenue makes millions by feeding our insecurities, scaring us into buying tons of unnecessary and sometimes downright harmful chemicals: deodorants, beauty aids, toxic dyes to color our hair so our gray won't show. It doesn't make sense. It's time to love ourselves just as we are, to see our Goddess-like beauty, and to reclaim a sense of ourselves as the sacred bringers in of life, not just because we are the childbearers, but because we are the nurturers, the unconditional lovers, the creators, and the keepers of a life-affirming culture.

This exercise will help. If you can get a group of friends together to do it, so much the better: support each other. Love each other's gray hair and wrinkles and weight. Glow with the energy of the Goddess. If you are ill and doing this exercise, work on loving yourself even though you are ill. Love yourself *because* you are ill. Love yourself.

If at all possible, use a Tarot deck that reflects a respect for women of varying races and body types. Mix the cards face down as you breathe deeply and fully. As you mix the cards, begin to imagine. Imagine how you would walk if you were a Goddess. Imagine how you would feel. Imagine every inch of your body glowing with sacred energy.

Now begin to choose cards. These will be pictures of the sacred energies that you embody—because you *are* Goddess. Negative cards, which are often graphic depictions of our negative self-image, are recognized and then put aside. Choose as many or as few cards as you like. Touch each positive one to the specific area of your body to which you feel it corresponds and then place it down on your playing space in a pattern that is pleasing to you.

Recently, a colleague who had been feeling tired and frumpy tried this exercise. Here are her results, using the Motherpeace deck. She righted all reversals and read only positive cards.

She touched the Crone to her graying hair and the top

of her head, to honor the crone she was becoming and the old woman within who whispered such wise advice to her. The Six of Wands she touched to her lips, imagining speaking out from a sense of fiery personal power and Shakti courage. The Seven of Discs, with its image of a pregnant woman, she touched to her own rounded belly; she willed to see her shape as a sacred reminder of her own motherhood. The Eight of Wands, a picture of initiative and swift change, she touched to her feet, affirming a commitment to following her path and dancing her dreams. The Six of Cups, an image of strong emotion, she touched to her heart, honoring the honest expression of her feelings, however painful or scary. The Priestess of Wands she touched to her eyes, seeing herself as fiery and strong, able to walk her path with dignity, courage, and power. And the Ten of Discs, with its image of giving birth surrounded by a loving and supportive circle of women, she held in her hands, thinking of the many ways in which her creativity is supported by her sisters. When she placed this final card down, she realized that she had unconsciously made a spiral pattern with her cards.

BACK IN BALANCE

When we subvert our inner knowing by suppressing anger, grief, or any other strong emotion for a prolonged period of time, our wise bodies will react with pain, illness, and disease. Sometimes we can bring ourselves back into wholeness by simply recognizing and acknowledging the feelings we have suppressed. Sometimes those feelings will have to be honored and truly experienced in order to release them. For example, nobody wants to be stuck in anger forever—but if you've been swallowing yours for a long time, it may take a period of honoring your rage, giving it healthy and non-damaging outlet and expression, before you can move beyond it.

This Tarot exercise is meant to help you recognize where you are out of balance. Then you can regain your equilibrium by honoring your feelings and choosing food, teas, clothing, or scents to even things out—see chapter 3 for more information on correspondences.

First, mix the cards and then spread them out face down in front of you. Breathe deeply and fully as you hold your hands a few inches above the cards. Visualize a connection between your hands and the cards: it could take the form of beams of light or web-like strands of energy.

Now reach down and grasp the cards with both hands: pick up a good handful. Turn these face up and separate them into suits and Major Arcana. Now look carefully: are there significantly more of any one suit? Which one? What do the images on the cards tell you?

If you have a great many Major Arcana, know that this is an important time for you, a sort of crossroads where powerful forces surround you. Align yourself with them by learning more about them and by inviting them more fully into your life.

Many Cups: issues of emotion. Reversed, they are often an indication of repressed feeling.

Many Pentacles: issues of bodily wisdom. Reversed, they may depict a refusal to listen to the body, sluggishness, being out of touch, a lack of grounding.

Many Swords: issues of mental activity. Reversed, they may point to mental anguish or stress, mind-voices that won't be still, the mental hamster-wheel.

Many Wands: issues of energy and anger. Reversed, they usually indicate depression, anger turned inward, lack of energy, or lethargy.

We begin to get a clear picture when we put this information together. For example, a friend who tried this exercise reported that she received four reversed Pentacles and five Swords, which she interpreted to mean that she had lost touch with her body as a result of living too much in her head. Recognizing the inner truth of this, she decided to pay more attention to the messages of pain and stress that her body was sending her. She nourished herself with root vegetables and soothing broths, took time out a few days a week to soak in a bath with earthy essential oils, undertook a daily fifteen minute meditation to quiet her mind, and signed up for a full-body massage once a month. Two of the cards that she had drawn gave her images of serenity and physical well-being that fed her inner self; she placed them by her bedside where she could see them every night before going to sleep. Within a short time, she was calmer, happier, and in much less discomfort.

PICTURE OF THE PAIN

If you are uncomfortable in your body for any reason, this gentle way of recognizing and honoring your pain can be a great help.

Lie down comfortably. Close your eyes and mix the cards in a pile face down next to you, as you listen to your body. Do you have any pain? Is there tension or discomfort anywhere? What do you feel? Now, choose a card at random for each area of your body that feels out of balance, uncomfortable, tense, or painful. Place the card, face down, on that area—this becomes your Pain Card. Lie quietly for a moment, knowing that the images you are about to see will reveal something important to you about the nature of your pain and about your inner self. Now, pick up one of your Pain Cards and look at it.

The image you see may give you many different kinds of information. It may remind you of a childhood memory that you've repressed and that has begun to affect this part of your body. It may relate to a current issue that is giving you tension or stress, which has become stored in this area of your body. It may make specific suggestions for healing: the Motherpeace deck, for example, may yield the image of a woman receiving a massage, practicing different yoga postures, getting in touch with animal allies, or meditating in a safe space. Be open to the nurturing message your inner self sees in the card. Now place the card back on your body. Continue doing this until you have looked at all the cards you chose for yourself. When you have finished, close your eyes and lie quietly for a moment, knowing that your inner self has been heard.

HEALING ISSUES

The Picture of the Pain exercise above will often bring up a number of issues that may need to be healed or resolved in order for you to embrace your wholeness and feel better. This exercise is designed to help you begin. Depending on the nature or severity of your issues, you may want to enlist the help of a counselor or therapist as you do this work—but know that the Tarot, by communicating directly with your inner self, is already helping you to heal.

First, find the Pain Card that you chose in the preceding exercise that depicts the issue you want to address, or choose one now. Put this card face up in the center of your table or floor and spread the other cards face down in a circle around it, mixing them as you go. Now, look at the central card and concentrate:

Card 1 – Root. What image could help you to understand the roots of this issue? Turn over a card from the lower part of the circle at random and look at it. This card will give you perspective on the past, the factors in your personal history that relate to the issue.

Card 2 – Consciousness. What image could help you to become more conscious about this issue? Turn over a card from the top part of the circle at random and look at it. Making things clear to your conscious mind is an important part of healing. This card can help you to understand.

Cards 3 and 4 – Insight. What images could help you to resolve this issue? Turn over two cards, one from the left side and one from the right side of the circle. These cards will offer insight and clarity.

Cards 5 and 6 – Wholeness. What images could help to bring you into wholeness? Turn over two more cards, one from the left side and one from the right side of the circle. These are your healing cards, and if the pictures on them are negative, they are often graphic depictions

of what is wrong. Once you can see the problem clearly, you can begin to understand it and heal.

Here is how this exercise worked for a friend who tried it, using the Motherpeace deck. Feeling completely drained and depressed after a prolonged bout with Lyme disease, she drew the Shaman of Discs for her Pain Card. Puzzled, she decided to suspend judgment and put this card in the center of her circle of cards, wondering how this could possibly relate to her illness.

Her root card was the Two of Cups reversed. She acknowledged that, since she had been sick, she had been feeling unattractive and fearful of not being loved, of being rejected emotionally—a pattern established in childhood.

Her consciousness card was the Three of Wands reversed. Afraid to speak out, feeling blocked—again, an early childhood issue that had persisted periodically over the course of her adult life. After thinking seriously about the message of this card, she decided to be more courageous and begin to speak out about the issues in her home life that were bothering her, depleting her reserves of energy.

Her insight cards were the Son of Wands reversed and the Seven of Wands reversed. The Son card reminded her of how her illness was eclipsing her sexuality and vitality and echoed her childhood repression. And the Seven pictured her present feelings of powerlessness and insecurity, also reminiscent of childhood stuff. She recognized the pattern: her present lack of energy related to her recent illness, depressed her at least in part because it reminded her of similar uncomfortable feelings in childhood.

Her wholeness cards were the Ace of Wands and the Four of Wands. After being forcibly reminded by all these Wand cards that issues of energy and life-force were the primary concern here, she recognized the Ace, with its image of breaking out of the egg, as a powerful message of healing and hope. Opening her heart to the message of this card, she felt that her course of treatment would be successful, that she would eventually regain her energy and her zest for living—and that her experience would enable her to bring what she had learned out into the world in the form of an artistic project that had healing as its theme. The Four of Wands, with its emphasis on playful, youthful energy, was another reminder that her own liveliness would return and that the playful nature of the project she was gestating would help to bring a sense of fun back into her own life.

She finally understood her Pain Card: the Shaman of Discs pointed out both her own self-healing power and her ability to use her healing knowledge for the benefit of others.

SIMPLE GIFTS

This exercise is a simple way to find an image of hope and beauty with which to nourish your inner self, boost your immune system, and align yourself with your own inner wisdom.

First, lie down comfortably in bed with the cards face down next to you, on your strong side (that is, your right side if you are right-handed). Close your eyes and pay attention to your breathing, letting go of tension with every exhalation and visualizing healing energy entering your body with every breath. Mix the cards in a pile with your strong hand and imagine that healing energy is entering this hand from the cards. As you mix, ask the cards for an image that will cheer and heal. Then, eyes still closed, pick a card and hold it with both hands above your heart. Open your eyes and examine it.

If the card is negative or scary, honor the information it gives you about your dis-ease, then blow on it and send it to your other side, away from the rest of the deck. Continue to pick cards with your eyes closed until you find one that is beautiful, calming, or uplifting to you.

Now that you have your gift from the Tarot, really look

at it. Imagine yourself in the place or situation the card depicts. What does it feel like there? What does it smell like? What colors or sounds surround you? You can close your eyes and journey there in your imagination: give yourself this magickal healing vacation. When you are ready to return, open your eyes and take a few deep breaths.

Place the card where you can see it and be reminded of its healing energy, the healing energy that is meant just for you today. You may put it next to your bed or on a chest or bookcase nearby. You may want to place some fresh flowers or a crystal beside it—make a small altar to your own ability to heal and be refreshed.

COCOONING

Many parents have noticed that their children tend to come down with illnesses right before making a developmental leap: it's as if the illness gives the child a necessary time-out that enables her or him to progress. Thinking of sickness in this way may benefit adults as well; when we are mired in daily life, illness gives us a break so that we can make the next step in our development.

Many times, we use illness as a much-needed escape from the constant demands of work, family, and friends—for some of us, it's the only time we allow ourselves to rest, do nothing, have a little respite. Eventually, we learn to honor our periodic need for a time-out *before* we get sick. But whether we are ill or well, this exercise can be used to give ourselves the kind of soothing, nurturing rest we need.

First, make yourself some safe space: unplug the phone or take it off the hook, let housemates or family members know that you don't want to be disturbed for a little while. Feel good about setting these boundaries. Honor your inner lioness as she protects your self.

Now, get your favorite Tarot deck, lie down on your back, and make yourself comfortable. Close your eyes and mix the cards face down on top of your tummy. Then gently spread the cards all over you, as much as you can, making a cocoon of cards in which you can rest and transform. Stay quiet for a few minutes inside this protective, nourishing cocoon space. Take deep breaths and visualize yourself being held and rocked in strong arms, or imagine that someone large and loving is stroking your forehead. Bask in the loving, soothing attention you are receiving within your safe cocoon for as long as you like—you may even fall asleep for a little while.

Then, when you are ready, reach down and choose a card at random, with your eyes still closed: this is the opening in the cocoon, out of which you will be free to fly. Open your eyes and look at the card. If it is scary or challenging, file away the information it gives you and choose another until you find one that gives you wings, hope. Look at this card for a long time. Where will you fly when you're feeling better? What does it tell you about taking care of yourself? Hold its image with you when you return to the demands of your life. You may want to put it near the sink, on the refrigerator, on your desk or worktable—wherever you are likely to see it often and be reminded.

When you emerge from your Tarot cocoon, watch how the cards fall from you like dry leaves—or like pieces of a shroud. Take a deep breath. Feel free. Repeat this exercise as often as necessary.

BEDSIDE COMPANION

Being stuck in bed for a day or more can be a blessing—or a bore. This exercise encourages us to feel more playful around being bedridden. It doesn't take a lot of energy—you can do this even if you feel physically wretched—and it will cheer you up tremendously. People have cured themselves with laughter. It won't hurt.

Basically, this exercise gives you a bedside friend, someone to hold your hand and tell you jokes. And, unlike most of the human variety, this one won't care what you look like. No matter how long it's been since you washed your hair or brushed your teeth, your Tarot friend is there, nonjudgmental, jolly, and tireless.

And this is a *playful* friend. Remember hiding under the covers with a pal when you had sleepovers as a kid? That sense of secrecy and fun can be a help to you now.

Mix the cards face down and pick one at random. If it is negative or scary, put it aside and continue to pick until you find a card depicting a person who appeals to you. This will be your Bedside Companion.

First, really look at your Companion card. What does the figure on it look like? What is she wearing? What is she doing? Pay special attention to the colors of the card and the clothing—they may be helpful to you, embodying energies that you need more of in your life. For example, a predominance of green could indicate the need for a fresh start, a new beginning—or, on a more mundane level, more fresh greens in your diet. Let your inner wisdom have its say.

As you look at your Companion, try to imagine what she is like, how she thinks and moves, who she is. Now, close your eyes and breathe deeply and fully for a few moments. Imagine that your Companion is sitting on the bed next to you. How is she sitting? Cross-legged? In a dignified and elegant way? Sprawling? Sedate? What does she smell like? A Spring breeze? Mushrooms? Smoke? Seaweed? Sniff the scent with pleasure: you can smell where she has come from—perhaps a breezy seacoast, or the depths of a rich woods, or a dune baking under a hot, dry sun. She has come from a great distance to speak to you and share something with you.

Now burrow under the covers with your card: make sure your head is completely covered by the sheets. Hold the card to your heart and imagine that this Companion is saying

something marvelous and funny to you. You are safe together in a secret world. What does your Companion say? Does
she tell you a joke? Or a story? Does she sing you a song?
Take as long as you like to listen. Laugh if you want to. Your
companion may have a clever or goofy or bawdy sense of
humor. Enjoy it.

Now, with your eyes still closed, come out from under
the covers—your Companion has one more thing to give
you. It could be an idea. Or a recipe. Or a precious object.
Receive it with love. Then allow your Companion to return
to her special place, knowing that you can call her to return
whenever you have need of her. Open your eyes and say
goodbye to the card as you replace it in the deck. Remember
what you were given: if it is possible to procure it for yourself
in actuality, do it. If not, hold the memory as a special gift.

TEMPLE OF HEALING

Once, there were sacred places where you could go
when you were ill, places where wise and loving priestesses
encouraged you to sleep, and dream, and heal yourself. This
is a simple but very powerful exercise that makes a sacred
space of your sickbed, supporting your inner wisdom and
your strong powers of regeneration—in effect, a shrine to
your own inner healer.

First, make the bed as tidy and smooth as you like. If
you feel up to it, you may want to smudge it with a smudge-
stick or walk around it with a stick of incense that has a
pleasing scent to you. Then you may purify the bed with a
sprinkling of salt-water (see chapter 1, under "Purifying the
Space"), or you may put special stones or crystals around it,
or light a special candle nearby. Visualize your space becoming cleansed of pain or sickness as you do these things.

Now mix your Tarot cards face down in a pile and
choose four at random. If you find a negative or scary image,
honor it for the information about your illness that it gives

you and choose again until you find a card that feels hopeful, strong, and right to you. Take time to really look at each of your four cards. Let the images enter into you: close your eyes and "see" them with your inner eye.

Now place one of these cards at each of the four corners of your bed. They are your guardians, your protectors. Visualize yourself safe in the center of this sacred space. Lie with your eyes closed for as long as you like, surrounded and supported by your four Tarot guardians.

Leave the cards in their places for as long as you need them. Know that these Tarot images are feeding your inner self.

Visit with Your Inner Healer

Sometimes it can help to have an actual visual image, something to focus on, to recognize with both eyes and heart. This exercise helps us to give our inner healer a form—and although we know that this form is constantly changing and shifting, the shape it takes today is the one that will help us to feel better right now.

First, mix the cards face down in a pile. Then choose a card at random and look carefully at it. This is a picture of your inner healer for today. If it is a challenging or negative image, take a deep breath and relax: these cards are powerful teachers. How could this card relate to the way you feel today? If the card is just too uncomfortable, honor its information and choose again. Find an image that is nurturing to you.

Look at the details of the card for information about your own healing process. How can you bring the energies of this card into your life? Close your eyes and breathe fully for a few moments. Imagine yourself walking in a safe and beautiful place—in a Spring meadow, along the edge of a forest stream, on a warm sandy beach—wherever your heart wants to be. As you walk, feel the breeze, smell the wonderful scents around you, and know that you are journeying to meet your Inner Healer, who has been waiting for a long time to hold you in her arms. Now you see a special area in front of you: it could be a moss-covered stone shrine, or a marble temple, or a grove of trees. You walk toward it, knowing that your Healer is inside. As you enter, you see her: the figure from your card moves toward you and embraces you warmly, looking into your eyes and smiling with great humor and tenderness. Spend a few moments with her, knowing that she is a wise and powerful friend to you. She may speak to you or simply hold you in her arms. Take as long as you like to be with her. Then, when you are ready, say goodbye, knowing that she is a part of you and can be contacted or visited whenever you need. Take a deep breath and open your eyes.

You may want to place this special card where you can see it today: if you have already done the Temple of Healing exercise, add the Inner Healer card to the sacred space you've made of your bed.

SOOTHING TIME-OUT

It's no news that stress is a major factor in many of our ills and that our culture produces stress as a constant by-product, along with pollution and violence. We can break the cycle in our lives by recognizing the warning signs of a stress-attack, forgiving ourselves, and then taking loving, gentle steps to calm down. This exercise can help.

Actually, the simple repetitiveness and tactile pleasure of mixing the cards are soothing all by themselves, and continued play with the Tarot builds association with serenity and self-empowerment: before long, you will feel calmer as soon as you bring out your deck.

So, mix the cards face down, remembering to breathe deeply and fully as you do. You may want to close your eyes as you mix, allowing yourself to focus on the sensation of your hands touching the cards. When you feel ready, choose three cards at random and turn them over. Look for pictures of the problem, advice on remedying the situation, and general comfort.

An example: recently, a friend was at her wit's end after a long day of dealing with the conflicting demands of work and her housebound and cantankerous young son. Feeling her grip on herself and her patience slipping away, she ran into another room, pulled out her Motherpeace Tarot deck, and quickly tried this exercise, while listening with one ear for the sound of breaking glass or some other calamity. She drew the Two of Discs reversed: smiling wryly, she recognized this graphic representation of her feeling that she was losing her balance. Then she drew the Two of Cups, which she took as a lovely reminder of the closeness she and her son usually shared. Finally, she drew the Son of Cups reversed, which Vicki Noble defines as needing a time-out for rest or meditation or listening to soothing music, and which she felt was also an indication that her son was feeling out-of-whack himself. Already more relaxed and encouraged, she took a deep breath and rejoined her son, put some lilting Celtic harp music on the stereo, and offered him a foot massage. Soon both of them were calmer, happier, and having fun.

BEDTIME STORY

This exercise is especially helpful for children, but it will work for adults, too—find a loving friend or family member who will do this for you. Whenever we're sick, it can be extraordinarily comforting and restful to return to our child-selves. Having a dear one tell you a healing bedtime story may be just what the Wise Woman ordered.

Allow the child (or adult) to look through the cards until she or he finds one that is especially appealing. You may have the child describe the card in detail to you—pretend that you can't see the card and must be told what it's like. Then make up a short story about the figures or animals or objects in the card, incorporating as many of the details as you can. This doesn't have to be great art, just a soothing, simple tale that emphasizes love, serenity, and strength. Include the child in the story, if you can: interaction with powerful Tarot images is a healing experience. The child may want to hold the card and look at it while you tell the story.

We cannot always prevent illness or pain from disrupting our lives. But, with help from the Wise One deep inside us, the healing and enriching images on the cards, and enough loving nourishment, we can embrace the totality of who we are, ill or well.

FIVE
Creating

When we were small, before our teachers or our families or our culture spoiled things, we were *all* artists. Now we can begin again—by playing with Tarot to uncover that fearless and creative child we all once were, we can rekindle the sense of wonder, freshness, and joy in creating that is our birthright. With Tarot as our inspiration, we can revel in paints and clay and pencil-and-paper, get our hands dirty, make wild and thoughtless art, free verse, enjoy the liberty of expressing ourselves without the cruel and hampering voice of the inner critic canceling out our enjoyment. Tarot work takes us to a place deeper than the critic and makes us feel safe there. And when a Tarot card becomes the muse that inspires a poem, a painting, an activity, a song, a clay statue, or a ritual, we make a connection with that card in one of the deepest ways possible. Pleasure and healing and connection all circle together—because to make art is to make ourselves. When Tarot is our guide and companion in creativity, we make ourselves whole. Self-expression and self-healing are one.

This chapter is meant to get you started, suggest ways to approach the cards as keys to your own creating, get your sense of fun and desire to make things flowing together, and open your eyes to the possibilities that exist when Tarot and self-expression join hands. Feel free to try any or all of the activities, keeping in mind that a warm-up is usually helpful: you may find that the exercises will be easier and more fun if you do them after you have already done some Tarot work of other kinds.

TAROT-INSPIRED ART PLAY

FIVE STEPS TO TAROT CREATIVITY

I f you have been working much with the cards, you will often find that there is one that just keeps appearing again and again for you. Hard to ignore when it pops up over and over, you may want to honor its repeated appearance by making it the subject for something tangible, created with your own hands, as a way of saying, "Okay, I get it, I'm listening." In the process of doing your project, you just might hear what the card wants to say to you. It's a fine starting place. Once you have tried some of these suggested activities with this card, you may feel free to try them with any of the others. These exercises can be extremely powerful if you want to bring the energies of a certain card into your life. Choose the one you need—and start playing.

1. Copying

First, mix the cards face down in a pile and then turn them over one by one until you find the card that has been haunting you. Put it in the center of the pile and really look at it. Notice the colors, the shapes, the figures or objects on the card. Look at the clothing and details in the card, the relationships between objects and spaces. Imagine the texture of the scene: if you were in the card, what would it smell like? Would there be a breeze? Would it be warm or cold? What animals or birds would be living in this landscape? Would they be friendly to you? One way to pay close attention to the details of your card is to copy it on a photocopy machine, then paste it on cardboard, and color it yourself. Or you may want to draw the copy yourself, using whatever medium seems to work best, enlarging it if you want to.

After you've done the copying exercise, you may want to wait awhile before going on to the others suggested here. Allow the images of the card to penetrate your consciousness.

2. Coloring

Once you have the details of the card firmly in your mind's eye, you can begin to play. Place the original or your copy of the card in front of you, grab a sketch pad and some crayons, markers, colored pencils, or paints, and make some splashes of color on the paper. They can echo the colors of the card or represent your feelings about the card. Don't try to make them "look like" anything: these are just abstract shapes in color. Have fun with this: get sloppy, go off the paper—neatness doesn't count unless you want it to.

3. Moving

Now really notice what these colors and this card make you feel like in your body. Do they make you want to stroke something? Pound something? Kick, roll, dance, stand quietly? Whatever you feel, try doing it for a while and know that you are embodying the energy of the card as you experience it.

4. Writing

Now write down how the card makes you feel, what it reminds you of, how it relates to your life. Free-associate, using the images on the card as your starting place. Include as many sensory details as possible. Try writing a poem from the point of view of the figure in the card or from that of one of the animals or objects in the card. Place both the original card and its copy face down at the end of this exercise.

5. Creating

The final step, when you feel ready, is to design your own version of the card. This will not be a copy but will be your unique and personal way of seeing the card. You may want to include the colors, motions, images, and ideas that the preceding exercises gave you. Remember that nobody is grading you on your work—this is just for your own pleasure. Use any medium that appeals to you: if paints or pastels aren't your style, you can make your embodiment of the card out of clay or carved wood—anything that works for you. If you don't want to draw, paint, carve or model the images yourself, cut out pictures from catalogues or magazines and make a collage. You may want to place yourself in the card: use old photographs (or photocopies of them). You don't have to stay true to the shape of the original card if you don't want to, and you can make the card as large as you like. You may want to include personal details—a sense of who you are and what the card means to your life—or you can make this a more objective vision of the card. Have fun with it. Put on some trancey music. Sing as you play. Be as messy and idiosyncratic as you like. This is just for you (unless you choose to share it).

When you have finished, congratulate yourself. Display the card where you can see it often: it may become the focus for an altar or shrine. Your friends may want to try the exercise, too; share your results together. Remember that this is a mutual exploration of the inner self, not an art exhibit. There are no wrongs or better-thans. Be proud of your unique and individual expressions of the cards.

Once you've started, you may go on to do a series of paintings, poems, or other creations inspired by the cards that are most meaningful to you. The following quick but significant exercise, a sort of distillation of the more detailed work you did above, can help you to loosen up and give you some ideas and inspiration for other work around the cards.

TAROT PAGE

Choose a card at random, or find one that seems especially meaningful to you. Examine it carefully. Now, using a
large sheet of cardboard or sketch paper, begin to write
down a few images and words about the card. You can write
the words any way you like: along the edge of the page,
upside-down, whatever. Now free-associate, using those
images as your starting place. Scribble the words as quickly
as you can. Try spiraling around the central word or writing
phrases like rays from a central sun. Next, make some swirls
or strokes or explosions of color, however the card makes
you feel. Think wild: if it is a Pentacle or Disc card, you can
use mud; singe the edges of the paper for a Wand; watercolors are a natural for a Cup card, and so on. You may want to
include your handprint (the most personal of maker's marks)
or put some heavy lipcolor on and press the paper to your
mouth. You can mix your saliva with chalk or dry paint, or
use your menstrual blood (see chapter 6 for more on honoring your bleeding times with Tarot). The important thing in
this exercise is to make a physical connection between your
whole self and the card.

You may include tiny detailed sketches, or cut-out photographs, or seeds from the orange you just ate, glued on.
Anything goes, as long as it makes some link with the card—
the more you play with this, the more inventive you will
become. Poke a hole in the paper and stick a weed or a
feather through it. If the card reminds you of someone,
include her or his phone number or glue on scraps of fabric
from old clothes or bits of an old love-letter. If the card
reminds you of a famous poem, include a few phrases. If it
reminds you of a dream, write it out or draw a quick picture
of it. None of this has to make logical sense, as long as it
feels right: this exercise is a vacation from intellect. But after
you've finished it, you may want to ask yourself what you
learned about the card from doing it, and what you learned
about yourself.

This Tarot Page exercise allowed its maker to express her personal vision of the Nine of Pentacles, even though her last artistic effort using markers, paint, and glue was a peace poster done in 1970! The discs she used to symbolize the Pentacles are photocopies from the unbelievably wonderful Goddess amulet divination set created by Nancy Blair, entitled *Amulets of the Goddess: Oracles of Ancient Wisdom* (Wingbow Press, 1993).

If you do this exercise more than once, you may want to staple or sew your finished pages together. Then you can consult your Tarot Book whenever you want ideas for a project with a card as its theme.

Honoring the Card

Sometimes you may feel like doing something creative around a card but you don't know what, exactly. In this case, try allowing the card itself (speaking with the voice of your inner self) to tell you what it would like. You may not think of yourself as a painter or poet or dancer, but the card and your inner wisdom know what you can do. Trust your own powers and see what you make. Practice in creative visualization will make this exercise easier to accomplish.

Choose a card at random and examine it carefully. Then close your eyes, breathe deeply and fully for a few moments. Picture yourself walking along a beach, or down a candlelit corridor, or down a rabbit hole—and when you are ready, allow yourself to step into the card. Imagine what it would feel like and smell like there. Look around and notice the details that surround you. Approach the central figure or animal in the card and greet it. It may have something to give you or something to say to you. After you have visited for a while, ask it how it would like to be honored. Would it like you to write a poem about it? Would it like you to do a dance that evokes it? A pattern drawn in sand? A painting that will hang in a special place? When you are ready, slowly come back to your ordinary awareness—breathe deeply and fully for a few moments and then open your eyes.

Now do what the card has suggested. Approaching your creative activity in this spirit of reverence and honoring is a great key to unlocking your gifts and your joy in creating.

UNCONTROLLED ART—LETTING IT HAPPEN

When we relinquish control and let magickal accidents happen, the results can be just as synchronous and exciting as the apparently random but profoundly meaningful patterns of the cards. In other words, you can do art in the same way as you play with the cards: by closing your eyes and allowing random events to shape your work.

There are many ways to go about this, but relaxing and allowing yourself to let go are the keys here. Put on some soothing or meditative music while you play. Drink some mugwort tea. And prepare to be surprised.

First, choose a card at random and place it face up near your playing space. Really study it for a few minutes. Then close your eyes and allow your hand to doodle on a piece of white paper with a white crayon. Next, dribble or brush on random splashes of paint. You may blot it with scrunched-up tissue, or blow on it to move the paint, or hang it so it drips. (You could try using mugwort tea to wet your watercolors, or adding dried mugwort to your tempera.) After the painting has dried, take a deep breath and see what has appeared. You may want to half-close your eyes and turn the paper around so that you see it from every possible angle. Are there any connections with your card? Or does your painting remind you of a different one? Very often, shadowy shapes reminiscent of the images on your card will form as if by magick. You may want to use colored pencils, markers, or crayons to make these shapes more distinct.

A similar effect can be obtained by brushing on rubber cement in random patterns, painting over it, and then rubbing off the cement after the paint has dried. Or you can try the ever-popular ink-blot effect, using large wet drops of watercolor or tempera paint, folding the paper while the paint is still wet, and unfolding it to see what appears.

Dabbing blobs of acrylic paint on glass, pressing another piece of glass or a sheet of plastic wrap on top, and then removing it will also cause some wonderful patterns and textures to develop on their own; some of the great surrealist artists used techniques like these to shape their work, allowing the beneath-the-surface forces to decide what the form would be.

You can invent other ways to allow accidental art to happen around the images of the cards. Do a painting with your eyes closed and then hang it outside in the rain. Put paint on your feet and dance on the paper. Take a walk and pick up the first ten portable items you find and glue or tie them together. Then stand back and see the connections with card images. After a lifetime of striving and making things happen, it can be a profound experience to simply let go and watch.

Poems, paintings, and other works that we normally think of as "art" are all wonderful to do with the cards in mind, but there are lots of other, less conventional creative projects and activities just waiting for you to come and play. Here are some specific examples, just to give you an idea of the realm of possibility, using three Motherpeace cards as inspiration. You may use the definitions of the cards as springboards to your imagination or simply allow the images to inspire you. Either way, your play will be meaningful.

The Star

- Take a long bath and float real flowers on the water. As you bathe, picture all your worries and troubles being gently and lovingly washed away. Remind yourself that you are a child of the Goddess, that you deserve blessings and joy in your life.

- Make a wreath of paper flowers (like the blue morning-glories that wreathe the bottom of the card) and wear them. Imagine that you are Mother Nature's daughter (or son) and go for a walk in the most wild and natural spot you can find.

- Dig a small pool in your yard and line it with rocks. Fill a jug with water, like the one in the card, and pour it into the pool, then watch as the water soaks into the earth. Keep the rock-lined hole in the earth as a reminder of the card and observe it after rainfalls.

- Make a tiny green frog from clay or dough, like the one that sits on the central rock in the card. Carry it with you and pretend that it croaks words of wisdom in your ear, affirmations like "You deserve to be happy."

- Next time it rains, go outside and let it wash away your cares. Dance. Feel renewed.

- Paint a picture from the point of view of the eagle that flies in the upper part of the card: put yourself in the pool and observe what you look like to the eagle. Then imagine that you have become the eagle and let your spirit soar. Look for feathers outside and keep them where you can see them often and be reminded of your own power to fly.

- On a warm night, go outdoors, lie down on a blanket, and look at the stars. Find one special star and really gaze at it for awhile. This is your star. Make a wish on it. Name it. Imagine what it would look like if it had a human shape. Look for it in the sky for several nights, or throughout several seasons, and see where it travels.

The Eight of Discs

- Invite your friends over and have an arts and crafts day together, everybody doing their own thing, but in community, like the women in the card. You will find that it's a lot of fun to create together. Share ideas. Make beautiful objects that you will use in your daily life: a bowl, a mat, whatever you can imagine. Support each other in your desire to make every aspect of your lives both beautiful and meaningful.

- Design a personal mandala—a round disc covered with patterns that are significant to you—like the ones on the card. Paint it or use dyed sand or crushed weeds and flowers to color it. Have a reason for every color and pattern you choose: what do they say about you? How do they embody qualities you would like to invite more fully into your life? Place it where you will see it often.

- Take an entire day and do all of the household tasks you would normally do—cooking, washing dishes, tidying—but do all of them mindfully. Try to be conscious of the importance and sacredness of your work. Ask yourself how you can make each chore more connected to your inner self. Take off your clothes and sweep naked. Sing while you dust. Feel that every step you take around your living space is putting sacred energy into the floor. For more on this, see the section on everyday rituals later in this chapter.

The Three of Cups

- Put on some music that makes you feel alive and happy, and dance. Invite your close friends over to dance with you. If any of you play musical instruments, have a jam session. Then hold hands and dance in a circle until you've danced yourself into a magickal, joyful trance.

- Take a notebook and pencil with you and find a stream, if there is one nearby. Sit with your hands or feet in the water, imagining that this is the magickal spring of inspiration. Really allow yourself to feel the flowing power of the water. If it is drinkable, cup your hands and sip some. If not, splash yourself. (If there isn't a stream nearby, place your hand under a running faucet for a few moments and imagine that the Goddess has bewitched your water, magickally inspiring all who drink of it.) Imagine that you are now filled (or cloaked) with inspiration. Then pick up the pencil and write down the first words that come into your head. Don't think about it—just keep writing. Simply record whatever you hear in your mind, even if all you hear is, "I can't do this." Keep writing for at least fifteen minutes or longer. The more often you do this exercise, the easier it gets.

• If you had a winged horse like the one on the card, where would the two of you fly? Make a simple map. Close your eyes and do a creative visualization of your journey. Imagine what it would feel like to sit on the back of a flying Pegasus—the horsey smell, the wind beating against your skin, the muscles moving beneath you. What would your home, your street, look like from up high? Become the winged horse and feel the sun on your wings, the strength of your muscles. Make a small Pegasus figure from clay or dough, or paint a picture, or cut out a few images from magazines that evoke this feeling of powerful free flight. Make up a Pegasus song and sing it while you drive or walk. Dance a Pegasus dance. Find a plastic horse and glue wings on it and put it on your dashboard. Take a rubber duck and put a horse-head and wings on it and float it in your bathtub. Know that inspiration and the ability to soar in your imagination are always with you.

MAKING TAROT TALISMANS

There is yet another way that we can work with the cards creatively: by constructing talismans around them, we can answer specific needs, bring about certain desired states of mind, and empower ourselves. The term "talisman" refers to an object or collection of objects made with magickal consciousness to serve a specific purpose (it is sometimes also called an "amulet"). We may make talismans to feel protected, or to bring about healing or prosperity, or to make ourselves feel desirable. Other purposes, even more specific, could include finding a home or a job, being successful in court, or attracting a mate. Talismans are as many and varied as human needs.

Talismans in general are meant to bring about a desired state of mind in the person making it. They are *never* part of an attempt to coerce anyone else's will. (This is why you can make one to feel more attractive and lovable, but would not make one to get your next-door neighbor to fall in love with you. That kind of manipulation is dangerous and unethical.) Many wonderful things can happen when you align your inner self with the change you want and need. Making a talisman is a great first step.

Some talismans are carried: a personal empowerment talisman may be worn in a pouch around your neck, for example, or one for confidence in a job interview could be placed in your briefcase or hip pack. Others are kept in your home, hidden from sight (a home-protection talisman, for instance, may be tucked away in a closet or cupboard). Still others are placed where you will see them often and be reminded of your intention.

Here are a few simple steps to get you started. As with any other magickal work, the key is to stay open and receptive to your inner voice, your wise-woman impulses: if the Tables of Correspondence in chapter 3 say that you should use bay leaves in your talisman but you feel attracted to peppermint, use the peppermint.

First, be clear with yourself about your needs and release any guilty feelings that tell you such focus on the personal is selfish: it isn't. You deserve to be happy and to have what you need. Knowing this, believing this, is the real first step to making magick—after all, good things can't happen for you unless you allow them to. If you are a vibrant and joyful person, those around you are bound to be affected in a positive way. Your personal happiness is for the good of all.

Once you know what it is that you want to achieve, look through the cards until you find one that embodies or puts into picture form the desired outcome. For example, you might choose the Ten of Cups for a happy home, the Empress for bringing a creative project to fruition, any one of several Pentacle cards for prosperity, or the World for greater consciousness. Put the card you have chosen in the center of your working space.

Next, find a container to hold your talisman. You may want to house it in a pouch, or a small bowl or bottle, or an envelope, or a small carved box—whatever feels right to you and fits the intended final location of your finished product. If you plan on wearing the talisman, for instance, you'll need to keep it small and light, but you can be unconventional here: if hanging a pouch around your neck doesn't strike the right note for you, consider putting your talisman inside a cotton menstrual-pad holder and wearing it that way (this would be perfect for a talisman to make you feel more sexually aroused, for example).

What suit is your chosen card? Or is it one of the Major Arcana? Consult the Tables of Correspondence in chapter 3 to give you some ideas of possible ingredients that resonate with your card: dried flowers and herbs, nuts, seeds, and other non-perishable foods, small stones or crystals, feathers, shells, and on and on—there are infinite possibilities to consider. You may want to include the actual card in your talisman, or a copy of it. Once you have gathered and added a few ingredients that traditionally are associated with your talisman card, then you are free to get really creative. Once again, you can use anything that feels right—snippets of fabric, dabs of perfume or essential oil, cut-out photos or images from catalogues or magazines, found objects that have personal significance to you. Have fun with the process, keeping your desired outcome in mind in a positive and affirming way throughout.

When you've put everything you can think of in your container, you will want to close it and put a magickal seal on it as a way of telling your inner self that the talisman is finished, closed, and protected—and ready to begin working for you. This can be accomplished in several ways. You may melt some beeswax and seal the bottle, box, or envelope with it. You may spit on it (this may sound a little disrespectful and disgusting, but body fluids make a physical connection with your work and have been used for centuries in magickal work for precisely that reason). You may tie it with a piece of string, knotted a few times; as you knot, visualize your outcome as an accomplished fact. You may take a deep breath and then exhale over your talisman. You may place your hands over it for a few moments, picturing that it is sealed and beginning to generate power. You may combine some of these ideas or make something up that feels right to you. And always be sure to follow up the making of your talisman with some concrete, physical-plane action: support your talisman's work for you.

Once your talisman is closed and sealed, you will want to keep it that way. Then, after the desired effect has been attained, it is a mark of respect for the power of your inner self to carefully open the talisman and scatter, burn, or bury the ingredients, with thanks.

Some months ago, a friend decided to make a Tarot-inspired talisman for finding a Full Moon group. A long-time solitary follower of the Goddess way, she felt ready to celebrate and share with like-minded others. She chose the Motherpeace Ten of Cups, a beautiful depiction of joyous community and communion with Source. She painted her own version of the card on a small piece of cardboard and placed it in a blue-and-green earthenware bowl along with several Cup herbs and stones. She also included eggshells (to symbolize her hatching out of the solitary egg), a small rainbow decal (to echo the rainbow in the card), a piece of candlewax from her last solitary ritual, and a picture cut out from a women's spirituality magazine of women dancing in a circle together. She placed her hands on top of all this for a few moments, visualizing the talisman sending out a call to other women in her area who were committed to the Goddess, sealed it with her breath, put it on her altar, and then immediately placed an ad in the networking section of the magazine from which she had taken the picture. Within two moon cycles, thanks to the ad and two apparently "chance" meetings, she was dancing with a group; she brought her bowl to their first Full Moon gathering and burned the ingredients in the central fire while the women all sang a song of magickal sisterhood

TAROT RITUALS FOR EVERY DAY

We have already seen how doing a short preparation ritual can deepen our experience with the cards. But Tarot also suggests ways to create simple everyday rituals that give greater depth and meaning to the ordinary rhythms and patterns of our lives. By infusing the little moments with sacred consciousness, we honor our selves and our connection to all life in a profound way.

Most of us unconsciously create little rituals for ourselves anyway—it seems to be an innate human trait. Some of us can get pretty grumpy if our personal ritual patterns for the day are tampered with (a phone call before our morning cup of coffee, for example), and children, especially, seem to crave the security and comfort of a life filled with repetition. Imagine the effect of engaging your consciousness in the ritual-making that you already do!

So here is a method for bringing the sacred into the pattern of your day and creating small and beautiful reminders of your own wholeness and holiness. You don't need to do all of your rituals all of the time (although you may want to take an entire day and try living it ritually, with grace and unfailing consciousness). Sometimes, a few moments of focused awareness in a week are all that is needed to reconnect you to the depths and heights below and above you. Simple acts of reconnection, no matter how infrequent, are the basis of both personal and global healing.

First, think about the pattern of an average day—you may want to write a list of the things you normally do. Now try to see your activities by the starlit vision of your inner self and of the cards. What is the real purpose behind what you do? In what way could your inner self be allowed to speak or be involved?

Here are some examples, to start you thinking:

1. Get out of bed. Most of us can't start our day without this. Getting up in the morning is our daily living-out of Ace energy: freshness, new beginnings, the opportunity for action, growth, new possibilities. Try placing an Ace card near the bed and invoking its power when you awake. Echo the card with your body. The Motherpeace Ace of Wands, for instance, shows a baby hatching out of an egg, arms held wide—imitate this posture when you rise. Light a stick of incense to connect with air, or a candle for fire. Imagine that your morning mug of tea is the Ace of Cups encouraging you to dive in and drink deep. Greet the sun: it came up again! Put the Sun card near a bright window and gaze at it as the light warms your skin.

2. Shower or bathe. A great opportunity to do a self-purification ritual, allowing yourself to feel cleansed and radiant. The Motherpeace Star card or even the Motherpeace Nine of Cups, which shows several women lolling luxuriously around a pool (a sort of magickal spa), would make lovely images for nurturing your spirit while you bathe or shower. Sing your commitment to living life in partnership with your inner Wise One. Let all the old negative conditioning just flow on down the drain. When you step out of the tub, picture yourself glowing with Goddess energy.

3. Get dressed. Is there a court card that you would like to align yourself with today? What magickal persona or aspect of your own wonderful, multifaceted self would you like to manifest? Choose your colors and clothing with awareness. Chapter 3 gives lots of ideas. Feeling low? Wear something as warm and sunny as a Wand card to pick up your spirits. Need to feel more empowered? Wear purple. As you put on each item of clothing, say a few words about its significance to you: "These green socks to help me walk in balance with the green earth. This pair of red undies to celebrate my sensuality. This striped blue-and-red dress, like the Motherpeace Shaman of Cups, to help me remember my power to heal and transform emotion. This red vest, like the Priestess of Discs, to remind me to eat healthy, nourishing foods and to nurture my children with loving and grounded energy." Making a ritual of clothing yourself in Tarot images like these is a magickal key to self-empowerment.

Even though we tend to equate ritual with elaborate trappings—candles, incense, and the like—all that is truly required is mindfulness. As you move through your day—eating, feeding your children and companion animals, doing chores, or going to a job outside your home—you can ritualize each action by simply becoming aware of its significance. Oh Shinnah, a great Native American teacher, says that city sidewalks are made largely of ground-up and crushed quartz crystals and that we can program these crystals with every step we take, by walking consciously, sending feelings of peace and healing down through our feet. Imagine yourself and thousands of other people, trudging down the sidewalks of our huge cities on the way to work, all consciously sending peace into the pavement. Imagine, when you take your morning walk around the block, that you wear green to echo the earth and that you become conscious of her blossoming Empress energy with every step you take—that you twine a vine around your arm and honor your own vitality and flexibility. Imagine placing a bowl of earthy Pentacle food in front of your child with conscious awareness of its nourishing and grounded spirit, inviting that earth-spirit into your child, breathing your own blessings into it. Imagine that every new beginning you undertake, every project you complete, every loving or empowering act you commit, resonates with what you have learned of the Tarot. See yourself not only surrounded by the energies and wisdom of the cards but beginning to embody them. Imagine that you unplug your phone in honor of the Crone, so that you can have quiet in which to hear her wisdom: place that card on the receiver as a reminder. Imagine, as you drive your car, that you are becoming the Chariot, able to attain your goals: place that card on the dashboard. Imagine, when you put out food for the wild things who share your neighborhood, that you are inviting their energies into your life, like the Motherpeace Strength card, surrounded by animal allies: place that card in the window where you will see it as you watch the birds at their seeds. Sing it. Or say it. Or keep it silent in your heart, knowing that your choice to engage in this partnership with Tarot is already working a powerful and transformative magick on your life.

SIX
Celebrating

Every day may often be a special day as well: a day for celebrating a birthday or other milestone in our lives or a day to honor our cycles, the bleeding times that punctuate our lunar rhythms. Or today may be one of the key times of the year—equinox, solstice, or cross-quarter day—when the larger forces that move our planet are strongly felt, the earth's mood shifts, and we have the opportunity to align ourselves with her.

Tarot images are great sources of inspiration on these special days, adding their centuries-old aura of mystery and wisdom to our personal and planetary festivals, giving us rich and evocative ideas for marking these special occasions, and reminding us of our individual connection to the numinous.

The cards immediately give us a sense of the larger picture and the real significance of our celebrations. When we allow the Tarot to suggest activities, images, and even food and drink for our festivals and personal holy days, we add tremendous richness and depth to our experience, making a circle of wholeness that encompasses all the facets of our lives.

TAROT FOR BIRTHDAYS

*B*y reclaiming our birthdays as sacred, we give real significance and meaning to what is all too often a day of mourning and loss. By turning to the Tarot as a source of nurturing and affirmation, we can feel good about aging, undoing the harm of the cultural message that women, particularly, are only valuable (if at all) when young.

By encouraging ourselves to feel wise, feisty, and deeply beautiful—because of, not despite, the external signs of our growing older—we will give our daughters something many of us never had: living lessons on how to age, not only with dignity or grace, but with power.

Here are some ideas for Tarot activities that will help us give back to our birthdays the feeling of joyous festivity we can remember from childhood. Another year of learning, deepening, and growing in wisdom and strength is a true cause for celebration!

BIRTHDAY SPIRAL

Mix the cards as you meditate on all of the years that you have walked on this planet. Then begin to place the cards, face up and one by one, in the shape of a spiral. Put down one card for every year of your age, starting in the center with year one and spiraling outward. If you are seventy-eight or older, use two decks. As you count out the years, see the correlation between significant events in your life and the images on the cards. The spiral shape will place certain years near each other: see the pattern your life-events are making for you.

When you reach your new age, kiss the card or sing it a song or wear it as a party hat for a few moments—whatever seems silly and appropriate. Then examine it for information about the coming year. If you are doing this with friends, you may all want to join hands around the spiral and sing "Happy Birthday."

BIRTHDAY QUEEN (OR KING)

When you have a birthday, allow yourself to be Queen (or King) for the day. Pick the court card that embodies who you want to be: if you choose to add a dimension of spiritual power to this activity, you may work with the Motherpeace deck and become a Priestess or Shaman.

When you have decided which card you want to be, recreate the costume as closely as you wish, paying special attention to color, feeling, and mood. Allow yourself to have fun, and as you dress yourself, remind yourself that you are good, wise, and powerful.

Invite your closest friends over to celebrate with you. Let them know who you are, and, if you exchange gifts on birthdays, encourage them to bring ones that might be appropriate: the Queen of Cups might love a special seashell to listen to; the Priestess of Wands might like a magic wand set with crystals and copper wire made just for her. Celebrate your special power and its significance for the good of the group. Your friends may take turns telling you all the things about you that they find special and valuable. Our culture does not encourage us to bask in approval; many of us find it difficult to receive heartfelt compliments with anything but embarrassment and loss of composure. You can change this today by smiling serenely, nodding regally, and saying, "Thank you, I'm glad to know that," after every complimentary speech.

Have a birthday feast with foods and drinks chosen with your court card in mind, being as imaginative and wild as you like—you and your guests may enjoy a Queen of Cups sea-vegetable stew eaten to the tape-recorded sound of waves on the seashore, or the Priestess of Wands could crank up the heat and serve a flambée. You may want to decorate your place with the court card theme in mind, encouraging family and friends to make a washable-marker wall mural or to bring special props or magickal things that fit.

As the culmination of the party, you could give a gift to each guest that is a reflection of who you are: the Queen of Cups may give a mystical watercolor painting or a dream journal for her friends to keep; the Priestess of Wands may give small drums or rattles and invite her guests to take a trance journey with her. It is good to remember that, when we become who we are truly capable of being, everyone benefits.

Another variation of this activity is to invite your guests to come as their favorite court card, too. Then, as you sit enthroned in their midst, each guest makes a magickal wish for you (sort of like the Good Fairies in the Sleeping Beauty story). Either way, have a wonderful, empowering birthday!

SHINING SUN

It is becoming popular to refer to a birthday as a solar return, since this is the day the sun returns to the position it was in when we were born. This birthday Tarot spread helps us to see the coming year in this larger perspective and reminds us not only of the perfect balance and harmony of the sun's circle, but of our own power to shine.

Sit on the floor and begin mixing the cards face down, spreading them around you as you do so: you will end up in the center of a circle of cards. Now take a few moments to imagine that you are a bright and shining light. Turn up a card that is directly in front of you and imagine that your light is illuminating it, bringing it out of darkness. This is your birth-month. Now move a little to your right and turn up another card, for the month that comes after your birth-month. Continue turning in the circle and choosing cards until you have twelve cards facing up, the circle is complete, and you are surrounded by shining images. Examine them carefully for information about the year before you. If you turn up any troubling cards, remember that these are meant to be taken as timely warnings rather than portents of inescapable doom; consider how you may change your present direction. After you have finished, close your eyes and turn slowly in the circle one more time: imagine all the other magickal cards and images that are waiting for your light to reveal them in the coming year.

If you want to take this image a step further, make yourself a Solar Crown to wear: using raffia, a grapevine wreath, paper ribbon, or any one of a number of materials for a base, you can then decorate your crown with golden ribbons, shiny trim, glittery rhinestones, and other costume jewelry. Make it as tasteful or as gaudy as your heart desires. Then put it on and go outside in the sunshine (or shine a lamp on yourself indoors if it's a rainy day), and look at yourself in a hand-held mirror. Enjoy your flashy brilliance!

BIRTHDAY WISH

When we were children, closing our eyes, making a wish, and blowing out the candles was often the best moment of a birthday. Now that we are adults, we have so much more power to make our wishes come true, but we often neglect the magick of this little birthday ritual. Here is a way to rediscover it.

Mix the cards face down in a pile as you concentrate on the one wish out of all the possibilities for your life that you would really like to come true—the one thing that is most important and vital for you at this time. Visualize this wish strongly in your mind; picture it already happening, a fact of your life already manifested. Holding this image firmly in

your mind, take a deep breath and let it go, blowing out
over the cards. Now turn one card face up. Look at it carefully: it will give you information on the best way to make
your wish come true—or it may counsel you to make another wish.

HONORING OUR BLEEDING TIMES

Once, thousands of years ago, our foremothers
gathered in a special cave or hut for a few days
out of every month and bled together; tribal
women, living closely and without artificial light, were in
sync with the cycles of the moon and with each other.
Taking a break from daily chores to share wisdom and stories, as well as the intuitive and magickal power that women
feel when they are "on their moon," was a wonderful part of
living in pre-patriarchal community.

Once, priestesses and shamans honored our monthly
blood, reverenced its sacred, healing, and life-giving properties, and regarded it as miraculous—the blood for which
nothing had to die, which was given freely with every lunation. How different it is for women today, stuck in cultural
conditioning that teaches us to be ashamed of our periods or
to regard them as a messy and tedious inconvenience.

It is time to honor our miraculous female ability to know
with the body, to access real knowledge and wisdom through
the body. It is time to reclaim the power of our sacred
blood, and the lunar time of greatest power and knowing, of
heightened psychic sensitivity.

The following Tarot activities are designed to help us re-
vision our moontimes, either alone or with others. By creating a community of powerful moon-women, we make a
statement on many levels: loving our bodies, our Goddess-
selves, each other. There are activities here for a young

woman's first menarche and for women entering cronehood. This distinctly female inner work is ancient and powerful: you may find that it awakens echoes from a very deep place in your psyche. The cards are natural companions as you travel there—they were conceived in that same deep place.

MOON CARD

The next time you are "on your moon," take some time to be alone, to be quiet, and to listen to your body. Find a place where you won't be disturbed and make yourself a nurturing nest, surrounding yourself with comfort: soft cushions, a pot of soothing herb tea, and objects that are beautiful and significant to you. You may want to include a red flower, an opened pomegranate, or some other menstrual image. One friend decorates her blood nest with red silk scarves. Another wears a special red dress that makes her feel powerful.

Bring your Tarot deck with you and hang out with it for awhile. You may want to line your nest with the cards so that they touch your body all around. Close your eyes and breathe deeply and fully for a few moments. Then reach down and choose a card at random. Hold it to your belly, your womb area, and then look at it carefully. What does it tell you about your moon-times? This image could be the focus for creative work that you do while you are bleeding. You may want to make your own version of the card (see Five Steps to Tarot Creativity in chapter 5) and use some of your menstrual blood to color it. You may also want to mark the original card with some of your blood. Then, the next time you menstruate, place this card where you can see it and be reminded. You can choose a new Moon Card every year, or you may keep this one as long as you bleed. Take time to meditate with the image on the card every time you menstruate.

FIRST BLOOD

A young girl's first menstrual period is an initiation. Unlike her male counterparts who have no such experience, this dramatic physical event marks her passage into young adulthood in a powerful and recognizable way. A first moon-time becomes the gateway into a new life as a member of the ancient and powerful lunar sisterhood; the young woman is ready to experience her sexuality in time, open to the potential of life that flows through all fertile women.

Many families choose to honor the newly fledged woman with special rituals, parties, and gift-giving, which restore to this sacred event the respect it deserves. If your daughter or friend is about to menstruate for the first time, or if a group of young friends have already had their first flow, you may want to have a gathering for her, or for them. (If you never had a First Blood observance of your own, you could get together with your friends and throw yourselves a special celebration. It's not too late!)

The young woman will want to take an active role in planning: some will want noisy, lively festivities; others may prefer something quiet with family members only; still others may want a more spiritual gathering, with a Circle ritual involving women of all ages. Once this basis has been decided upon, the Tarot can suggest themes and activities, just as for the birthday celebrations, based upon a Daughter card from the Motherpeace deck, a Page card, or even the Queen that the new woman wants to become.

One of the events of the gathering could be the young woman's choosing her first Moon Card. If the gathering marks the initiation of more than one person, the group could try the following simple, powerful activities, which will also work for women's groups of other kinds; each is a celebration of a woman's unique ability to know, deeply, with her body.

WOMB WISDOM

The young women sit in a circle with the deck in the middle and mix the cards together by stirring them face down in a pile. Then, at the same time, each participant chooses a card at random and holds it against her belly for a few moments, then places the card face up in the center of the circle. This card is her gift to the group, her own unique perception that she channels through her womb.

Now each participant chooses another card at random, holds it to her belly, and passes it to the young woman on her left: this is her womb-gift to that person. All participants share their insights and ideas about the cards and their significance.

BLOOD FLOWER

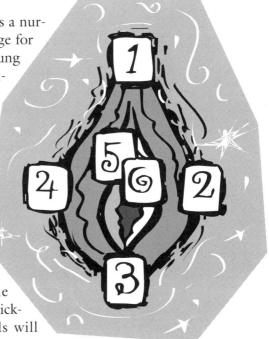

This activity provides a nurturing and magickal image for a newly menstruating young woman. If a group is celebrating together, each woman may make her own Blood Flower and share the results with the each others.

Mix the cards and lay them out in the following pattern:

Cards 1 – 4: These form the shape of the flowerlike vulva, the magickal gateway. These cards will give the participant information on her sense of the sacred and her relationship to her own emerging womanhood.

Cards 5 and 6: Like the sacred blood that she will bring forth every month, these cards represent her gifts that will nourish and empower the group—family, friends, community. These may be gifts of insight, inspiration, creativity, or personality, and they are her unique contribution.

The group will want to share their perceptions about the powerful nature of each young woman. The celebration may end with the giving of special gifts—such as a garnet necklace, a scarlet-covered journal, a red candle scented with patchouli oil—that will remind the young woman of her newfound power and encourage her to explore her own inner wisdom.

MOON CAVE

Every month, we are given the opportunity to make special magick, to celebrate and honor ourselves, our wise bodies, the Goddess energy flowing through us. The following activity may be performed alone or with other bleeding women; it gives us a way to recreate the sacred space where women flowered and flowed and made a womb of power for the good of the group. Our tribal ancestors knew what a reservoir of energy a group of menstruating women could be. The energy is still there: we are still channels for Goddess power in the world. Moon Cave recalls us to the wild and primal wisdom of our tribal roots.

As you mix the cards, visualize yourself sitting in a warm, darkened, firelit cave. The cave has shallow bowl-shaped depressions carved in its stone floor. Here you and your sisters give your lunar blood for the good of all. The cave is alive with energy and flickering firelight. You and your sisters may be dancing wildly in a circle, your bodies painted with sacred blood, or you may be quietly dreaming together. Visualize the cave as it feels best to you.

When you are ready, turn ten cards face up, one by one, placing them in a semicircle around you. These are the boundaries of your Moon Cave. Examine each one carefully—they will give you information on your needs and your abilities at this point in your moon, and the images will nurture you during your bleeding time. Notice where the cards fall in relation to you: what lies directly in front of or behind you? Which cards delineate the opening of the cave? You may pick up any card that feels especially meaningful to you and hold it next to your belly for a few moments. If you do this activity with a group, each woman may choose a few cards, placing them so that the group is entirely encircled with empowering Tarot magick.

While you are safe within the cave of cards, you may want to try some of the following moon-time ideas; there are many things we can do with our blood to remind ourselves of its mystery and power. Use it to paint or mark special crystals, jewelry, journals, your cards, your face, your body. Paint a picture with it. Water your plants with it. Put some in each corner of your home. Give it as a love-offering to a tree. Pour it over a stone, outdoors, in honor of the Goddess. Bleed directly onto the earth. Put some on a piece of cloth and carry it with you. Put a small bowl of it on your altar. Dip special rocks into it and then place them around your home or yard, or put them where you will see them often. Spread some on your hand and then make handprints on the wall. Dance on a large sheet of paper and allow your blood to flow from you with every step. Put a drop on your third eye and journey, or visualize, or dream—write down what you see. Find the card that embodies the way you feel today: are you feeling wild as the Motherpeace Daughter of Wands? Grounded as the Priestess of Discs? Honor your feelings.

CRONING

The Croning time comes when our monthly flow changes, lessens, and finally ceases altogether, when our physical selves begin to embody the inner Wise Elder, the Crone of power, who has been within us from the beginning.

Given our cultural conditioning, this is probably our most challenging time, the time when magickal encouragement is most needed as a reminder of our power and strength. Surround yourself with support: read positive and affirming books about menopause, about the Crone. Meet with other elder women and share your insights and experiences. And remember that the powers of intuition and the knowledge you have gained throughout your bleeding years have not deserted you—now, as Susun Weed says in her wonderful *Menopausal Years,* you will become She-Who-Holds-the-Wise Blood-Inside.

We have a vital opportunity here to recreate the respect and reverence due to the Crone, and the Tarot accompanies us on this vital journey to show us how. And for those of us who have lost our wombs to surgery, these simple Tarot activities can give us a way to bring empowerment and closure to the experience.

We usually begin to notice changes in our moon-times several years before they stop completely. To mark the beginning of this time of great discovery, we may choose a card at random to show us what we may expect as we begin our journey toward the Crone. Will our Croning be a time for gentle dreaming? Anger? Activity? Thinking things through? Tending a garden, writing, speaking out? The cards can give us a foretaste of the living-out of our natural inclinations when we no longer have to live to please others, when we embrace the freedom that accompanies our hard-won wisdom in such nourishing partnership.

Along with our many changes may come an inevitable sense of loss. As we move away from our role as Mother, we may mourn for what we leave behind. If you have stopped bleeding, either naturally or through medical intervention, then you may find the following ritual a healing and empowering way to honor your feelings. First, copy the Moon Card that you chose as a menstruating woman or do your own interpretation of it. Place this in the center of your space.

Now close your eyes and mix the cards face down in a pile as you meditate on the possibilities that did not reach fruition: miscarriages, abortions, works or ideas that never manifested. Choose a card at random for each of these, and after you have examined it, place the card next to the central Moon Card, forming a circle around it. Take the time you need to mourn their passing. Now pick up the Moon Card and hold it for the last time to your belly. Say goodbye to this symbol of the old self, the bleeding self. If you cry, mark the card with your tears. When you are ready, you may choose to burn it or put it away out of sight in a place that is special and sacred to you. Now pick up the cards that surrounded the Moon Card and place them behind you.

When you are ready, close your eyes again and continue to mix the remaining cards, beginning now to recall all that you have created. Celebrate your Mother Goddess ability to produce, to bring to birth—whether you focused on raising children or tending animals, nurturing a garden or a creative project, or pursuing a career. Choose a card at random for each child (actual or metaphorical) that you have birthed, placing each card face up in front of you. Open your eyes and see what you have chosen to mother in your life.

Hold your hands over these cards, noticing their brilliance and beauty. Feel good about your choices and the value of what you have nurtured. Now gather the cards together and place them behind you.

Close your eyes and go back into the dark one last time.

Mix the remaining cards, asking now what new life is about to emerge in you, as you leave behind your Mother self and become the Crone. Choose three cards and place them face up in front of you, then open your eyes and examine them carefully. Who will you become? What will you give to the community from your store of wisdom and experience?

Another way to celebrate your Croning time is to make yourself a Crone Crown with Tarot. First, make a simple base for your crown as you did with the Solar Crown for birthdays, using paper, cardboard, ribbons, raffia—whatever feels right to you. Next, mix the cards face down while you think about the gifts this new time will bring. When you are ready, choose five cards at random, then open your eyes and examine them. Any negative or scary images may be honored for the information they give you and returned to the pile; continue choosing until you have five cards whose images are pleasing and empowering to you. Use paperclips to fasten these cards to your crown (or make copies and staple them to the crown base) so that they form the upright rays of the crown. Wear your crown whenever you need a reminder of your value, wisdom, and strength.

TAROT FOR TRANSITIONS

The idea that we reach and incorporate certain important milestones in our lives is an ancient one. By consciously seeking out ways to ritualize these experiences with the help of Tarot, we invite the cards to be our inspiriting and helpful guides, magickal companions that illuminate our life transitions.

The following Tarot ritual ideas are meant to be starting places, central seed-ideas that inspire other related activities around these transitional life-events.

By creating initiation rituals that honor a boy's crossing over into manhood, we give him a sense of the sacred and an affirmation of his new status. But knowing exactly when to do this is a somewhat trickier proposition than with newly emerging young women, whose first bleeding clearly signals the time of initiation. Many of us choose the time of our sons' first nocturnal emissions (hence the name of this ritual) as part of a conscious choice to encourage a positive attitude toward sexuality. (And if your son doesn't announce the event—and most of them won't—the signs will be evident to the doer of the laundry.)

The activities that surround the following Tarot ritual can emphasize the importance of responsibility toward life. The gift of manhood is more likely to be taken seriously if it is treated seriously from its inception.

The young man is given his own deck of Tarot cards, which he has helped to choose previously. He then takes the deck to a private place (some young men camp out in the wild for several days; others hang out in the backyard for a couple of hours), opens it for the first time, and meditates on the cards. The following Tarot exercise gives support and guidance as he closes the door on childhood and reflects on the new life opening up before him. As with the First Blood celebrations, a young man may wish to share this initiation experience with several friends.

Mix the cards face down and then choose three Seed cards at random and place them face up. Examine them carefully. What would you like to plant in your life? What warnings or guidance do the cards give you at this special time? If one of the Seed cards has special significance for you, "plant" it at the bottom of the pile and choose another from the top of the pile at random to show the flowering result of your planting. You may choose to bring back the Seed and

Flower cards and share them with the group or with your family.

COUPLING

Whether we choose to celebrate a formal marriage or not, a couple's choice to commit, not only to each other but to the relationship, is a cause for celebration. Tarot adds its universality to a bonding ritual, which may be private, or part of a declaration of commitment in the presence of the couple's immediate community.

First, each of the two people chooses a card that represents her or him and then draws or makes a copy of it (for example, one friend recently decided on the Motherpeace Daughter of Wands for herself, and her lover picked the Motherpeace Priestess of Swords. Another couple might choose the Empress and the Knight of Cups).

Then, on the day of the ritual, the couple places their cards together, face to face, and twines the two cards with red thread. If others are present, this Couple Bundle may be passed around the circle and each participant may breathe a wish for happiness into the bundle. At the end of the ritual, the couple takes the bundle home and puts it in a safe place, where it can be a loving touchstone and reminder when times get rough.

BABY BLESSING

The following simple blessing ritual is a lovely gift for new parents and a beautiful welcome for the baby, with magickal wishes for her life.

The baby is placed in a basket or cradle in the center of the space, parents and celebrants enclosing the child in a loving circle. Pass the mother's favorite Tarot deck, or one that appeals to both parents, around the circle. Each participant looks through the deck, choosing a positive card as a blessing for the new baby, placing the card on the floor next to the basket, and saying aloud what she or he wishes for the child.

SEVERING

The ending of a relationship is often one of the most painful events we can face. Divorce, aside from its often harsh legal realities, takes place in a spiritual vacuum, with no thought given to the inner needs of the people involved. And nonconventional relationships, as well, need some way to give dignity and a sense of inner meaning to the passage of separation.

The following simple ritual makes a powerful visual statement: when we sever our bond with another, we take ourselves back again.

If possible, each of the two people makes a copy of a card that they feel is representative of them. If one of the former couple is unable or unwilling to take part, the other person will do both. Also draw or copy a card with an image of a happy, bonded relationship, such as the Rider-Waite or Morgan-Greer Ten of Cups.

On the day of the ritual, which may include friends and family or be completely private, place the copies of the cards that represent the couple in the center of the ritual space, with the happy-relationship card an inch or two above them, and a two-foot-long thin cord (made of a natural material) in a circle around this three-card grouping. With one hand, each member of the former couple takes one end of the cord, lifting it and pulling it taut. Then each takes a pair of scissors or a knife and simultaneously cuts the cord. If only one of the couple is present, she will do this herself.

If the couple made a two-card bundle like the one described in the Coupling ritual above, this may be used instead, cutting the red thread and unwinding it from around the cards.

In a bonfire, fireplace, or large bowl, burn the happy-relationship card and the pieces of the cord. Then each person picks up the card that represents them from the center of the space and puts it inside her or his clothing, next to the heart. (If only one is present, put the remaining card out of sight. It may mailed to the absent person at a later date.)

RETURN TO THE MOTHER

Most funerals, although an attempt to create ritual around death, are often lacking in spirit value. When we are grieving for a loved one who has died, the following simple act can be a comforting reminder of the cyclical nature of life.

Draw or copy a card to represent the person who has died. Choose a special place outdoors and dig a small hole. Place the card in the earth and cover it. As you do this, picture the earth as an all-embracing Mother welcoming back her child. Know that all who live on this planet return to her. None are lost.

You might want to plant a small flowering perennial over the spot and water it. Return as often as you wish to care for

it and keep it company. Watch its cycles. Sit beside it in all seasons. Mourn its passing in Winter. Rejoice in its renewal in Spring. And when you bring out your Tarot deck to play, rediscover the card whose copy you buried, still shining and fresh. Greet it with love.

TAROT FOR THE MAGICKAL ALTAR

The purposes behind making an altar are varied: to honor our concept of deity, of the sacred, and our own connection with it. To provide a focus for magickal work. To set aside a place for beauty and inspiration in our lives. To give comfort and solace in times of need. To rally the inner self toward a specific purpose or work or to give inner strength. To solve a specific problem or bring about a desired goal (similar to making a talisman), providing a special place to concentrate on these ends. And for fun—to celebrate the playfulness of our inner Wild Thing.

Whatever your reasons for choosing to set aside a consecrated space, know that humans have been doing this for time out of mind and that our continuing to do so today throws a loving line of connection back to the bones of our earliest ancestors.

If the idea of making a magickal altar is new or strange to you, you may want to reread chapter 1, or consult some of the books in the Suggested Reading list. But there is no great expertise necessary here: in order to make a special place to honor the numinous, you only need to follow your heart in every step of its construction. Tarot images make wonderful additions to any altar we make, so this chapter suggests several approaches, not only to making altars, but to playing with the cards in conjunction with your sacred space, allowing the Tarot to add its special power and magick.

First, you need to decide on a place for your altar. It should be sufficiently out of the way that it is safe and protected—and also so that you feel safe and protected when you visit there. If you have curious toddlers or companion animals—and breakable objects—you will want to put your altar out of their reach; and if your visitors are likely to ask prying questions, you will want to choose a private place so that you don't constantly have to explain or defend its presence in your home. Many of us have altars in our bedrooms or in the bathroom that guests don't use.

Next, look at the space you have available. Not all of us are fortunate enough to be able to devote an entire room to our altar or our inner work, but it's good to remember that we don't need to: an altar works perfectly well on one shelf of a bookcase, or on the top of a dresser or nightstand, or in

the corner of a closet or cupboard. And for those of us who love being outside, an outdoor altar made of stones or other natural materials could be a perfect choice.

If you have been working with the cards for any length of time and you know your basic Tarot suit and element, or if you have noticed that one suit predominates or attracts you, this could determine the direction in which your altar faces or the corner of your home or land that it occupies. Someone with a connection to Cups, for example, might choose a room whose windows face West or place the altar where she would face West when standing in front of it.

Once you've chosen the spot, the rest is easy. Let your creative spirit loose and have fun. Choose fabrics and colors that you like, which feel right or have special meaning to you. Ask your inner self what works. Ask the Goddess how she would like to be honored. Play with the things you have or make or purchase special altar objects. Many of us include something for each of the four directions: some examples could be a bowl of water or seashell for West; a rock, crystal, or dish of salt or dirt for North; a candle or oil lamp for South; and a feather or incense burner for East. Something from nature that echoes the current season—flowers in Spring and Summer, a bare branch in Winter, some bright leaves in Autumn—are also good additions, giving us a tangible connection to the natural forces around us. If you have a Power Animal—an animal whose special qualities are helpful to you or that makes frequent and meaningful appearances in your life—you may want to include a small statue or figure of it. And if you have developed a relationship with a particular concept of deity, then you will want to include a picture or statue. Or you may choose to omit any of these elements and include others simply because they feel right to you.

There are many pictures and photographs of personal altars in the Suggested Reading books. What you will notice is how amazingly different they all are: some are thickly crowded with yummy images and objects, while others are bare-bones beautiful. All are unique. If every element of your altar is deeply pleasing to you, you will have made it a unique expression of your personality. A natural consequence is that when you look at it, stand before it, you will immediately begin to feel peaceful, strong, uplifted—in touch with your center, your inner self.

Tarot cards make wonderful additions to a basic altar. The Major Arcana, especially, are images of great depth and magick that provide an excellent focus for meditation or magickal work, and the process of choosing one at random, examining it, and incorporating it into the sacred space becomes a sacred activity in and of itself. As you mix the cards, ask your concept of the Deeper Powers what it is that you need to learn, embody, or explore. Or ask your inner self which image would be of the most help to you right now. Choose a card with your eyes closed, place it on your altar, and open your eyes. How does it relate to the objects that surround it? What does it say to you about your life? Keep the card on your altar until you feel that you have understood or incorporated its wisdom, the lesson in the card that is unique for you at this time. (Some of us have been known to keep certain cards on our altars for months. Years, even. That's fine.) You may find that a particular Tarot card suggests actual objects to include on your altar as well; a chalice with a flower floating in it, for example, or a small bay wreath are both significant images on certain Cup and Wand cards.

Another valuable exercise involves choosing a card at random to tell you something about your relationship with deity—Goddess, God, whatever you conceive it to be. Place this card underneath the altar depiction of that deity or lean the card against it, so that you form a visual connection. Recently, a colleague tried this exercise and chose the

Motherpeace Magician: she leaned it against her small clay
Goddess, where they appeared to join hands. She thought
about this and meditated on it every time it caught her eye.
Eventually, she performed a solitary ritual before her altar,
recreating the props shown on the card as well as she could
and imitating the Magician's stance. Through doing this, she
finally understood the message of the card: she needed to
embody the Goddess in her own life by consciously working
magick, channeling powerful forces to change her life for the
good of all.

Altars are often used as a focus for the kind of life-chang-
ing work that was suggested by the Magician above. What
do you need to change? What issues need clarification for
you? What are some solutions to specific problems? Tarot
cards can give us a lot of valuable and helpful information,
providing positive and nurturing images that often contain
not only a clear picture but an empowering solution—either
magickal or amazingly specific and practical—to the prob-

lem. By asking yourself these questions, choosing cards, and then placing these important cards on your altar, you create a continual visual reminder and a focus for your inner work.

As a follow-up to choosing the Magician, the same woman asked, "What do I need to change, specifically?" and drew the Motherpeace Strength card tilted to the left (because the deck is round, cards can be tilted as well as reversed). She admitted some periodic feelings of weakness and dependency, and then she read Vicki Noble's commentary on the tilted meaning of the card: holding back, not wanting enough. She realized that self-esteem problems sometimes kept her from going after what she wanted most—a successful career as an artist. Next, she asked, "Okay, then, what do I need to do? What are the solutions here?" and chose the Empress, tilted to the right (struggling toward manifesting her creativity, according to Noble), and the Ace of Wands, a fiery image of bursting out of the egg, joyous liberation and rebirth of self. She placed the Ace card on her altar; and every time she felt passivity or depression creeping up on her, she looked at the card and felt both empowered and determined.

Tarot and your altar can also make a magickal partnership when you want or need something specific and are working toward bringing it into your life, allowing it to enter. By choosing cards at random to suggest ways to go about getting what we need, or to show us where we may be resisting its presence in our lives, we go a long way toward dissolving unconscious blocks to our happiness and creating the positive attitude that will enable us to move ahead. After you have worked with the cards asking these questions— "What may be holding me back in this situation? What do I need to know here? How can I best go about getting what I want?"—it can then be enormously helpful to choose a card consciously that embodies your desired outcome, just as in the talisman work in chapter 5. Place this card on your altar:

it will act as a magnet, clearing your consciousness and empowering you to draw what you want into your life.

TAROT FOR ALL SEASONS

For many of us seeking to find greater and deeper connection with the forces that move our planet, Tarot can be a valuable ally as we celebrate the important moments in our planet's yearly cycle. By first becoming aware of the existence of certain special days, and then by honoring them with Tarot images as well as with meditation and festivities of other types, we strengthen our bond with the great Mother.

We begin with an appreciation of the seasons and of the yearly pattern of birth, growth, decay, death, and birth again. By working with the cards to discover the underlying significance of each season for us individually, we connect with what is larger than self, finding new and meaningful ways to embody and celebrate the energies of the season and eventually recognizing the profound implications of the yearly cycle.

Here is a simple but powerful way to create your own personal seasonal connection. At the beginning of a season, choose one of the suit cards that corresponds to the season (see chapter 3) or another card that embodies the feeling of the season for you and place it on your altar. In doing this, we create a visual connection that also works in our inner selves, entraining us with the energies—the Earth's mood—of that time of year.

A friend chose the Ace of Swords to help her shake off the end-of-winter doldrums and harmonize with the freshness of Spring. She propped it up on her dresser, where it was guaranteed to give her a continual visual reminder: time to wake up! There may still be snow on the ground, but

Spring is nearly here! By the end of March, she was feeling re-energized and filled with new ideas for projects to see her through the Spring, a direct result, she felt, of the Ace of Swords.

Another way to experience the season is to choose the court card that corresponds to it and place it on your altar, imagining ways that you could embody this card in your life. In Autumn, another friend put the King of Cups on his worktable and realized that, for him, the card embodied creativity. He decided to stop putting off doing the painting that he loved, and by early October he was happily up to his elbows in oil paints and turpentine in every spare moment.

You might want to ask yourself who you would like to be this season, what marvelous Tarot quality you would like to embody. Then find a court card or other Tarot image depicting that quality or activity and put it on your altar, carry it with you, or place it where you will see it often. Make lists of ways in which you could manifest this card at this particular time of year.

The sheer beauty of Tarot images, when used consciously to awaken our response to a season, becomes a powerful key for greater alignment. And the cards can also serve to evoke the year's holy days, earth-sun conjunctions that make such important pauses in the ever-turning wheel.

It is important to remember that many of these festival days, older than human time, are really celebrations of brief moments, because the earth never stands still: in less than a heartbeat, less than the pause at the top of a breath, the moment of greatest light is over, the moment of perfect balance is gone, and we are whirled away for another year. By taking time to prepare for the moments, and by entering into their spirit and celebrating them wholly, we both lengthen and honor them, incorporating their special energy into our lives in a joyous and tangible way.

Here, then, are the eight major festivals of the year, the old quarter and cross-quarter days that all our ancestors knew, if not by these names, then by others just as ancient and traditional. Suggestions for cards that will serve to connect us with their spirit are given—but feel free, as always, to make the connections that feel right to you. You will find that the primal rhythm of these holy days speaks to our own cycles. We dance the earth-dance together: meditating on the card images, or allowing them to suggest simple ritual activities, helps us find our way back to Source.

Imbolc

February 2, honoring the visibly returning daylight and the stirring of the seeds beneath the earth. A time to put the darkness and cold behind us, to prepare for activity, to come out of hibernation. Choose images of beginnings or youthful energy: Aces, Pages, the Fool.

Wear something that you have made or chosen with an Imbolc card in mind. Go outdoors barefoot and feel the earth under your feet. Picture the seeds beginning to waken in the dark, unseen. Picture the ideas and events and projects that you are beginning to gestate in the darkness of your inner self.

Ostara

Vernal equinox, when day and night are equal in length, around March 21. Spring breezes begin to blow, heralding change, growth, and rebirth. Choose Judgement, to coincide with the Easter image of resurrection, or the Eight of Wands to align yourself with swift movement.

Get a small flowerpot, which you can paint or decorate if you want, and fill it with earth. Then choose a Tarot card that represents what you would like to help grow in your life. "Plant" it in the pot, so that it stands up. Place this where you will see it often.

Beltane

The great May 1 celebration of fertility and sexuality. Celebrate sensual pleasure, alone or with a loved one, and your own limitless power to create. Choose images of union, merging, fertile growth: the Empress, the Two of Cups, the Lovers.

Light pink flower-shaped candles and decorate your bedroom with fresh flowers. Place the Lovers card above your bed and meditate on its significance; allow yourself to become the channel through which immense and loving powers can flow.

Litha

Summer solstice, the longest day of the year, around June 21. The sun is at its peak of greatest power. Choose Wand images of positivity and warmth or (the perfect card for this day) the Sun.

Decorate a vine wreath with golden ribbons and marigold flowers in honor of the Sun or paint a big sunflower on your door. Visualize yourself like the child on the Rider-Waite Sun card, naked and unafraid, filled with joy and self-confidence, riding bareback on the horse.

Lughnasad

August 1, the festival of the grain and first harvest. Honor your power to bring things to fruition, completion. Choose the Four of Wands or the Queen of Pentacles.

Bake a loaf of bread. Light a bonfire and watch it as the sun sets. Choose several cards to represent your own inner harvest, and arrange them beautifully on an earthenware plate. Pat yourself on the back.

Mabon

Autumn equinox, when day and night are equal in length, around September 22. The final harvest: taking stock, giving thanks. Choose the Two of Cups to celebrate balance, or positive Pentacles images such as the Nine.

Cut an apple crosswise to reveal the Pentacle of seeds inside. Mix your cards face down and choose five at random, placing them face up in the same Pentacle pattern as the apple seeds. What will remain in your larder for the coming lean months? What do you have to be thankful for? Examine the cards.

Samhain

Halloween, the day to honor death and our own beloved dead, October 31. Best night of all the year to work with Tarot or any other form of divination, when the veil between the worlds is thin. Choose the Death card, or the Motherpeace Crone to honor our power to go within, to listen to our inner wisdom.

Make a shrine, indoors or out, to honor the Crone. On it, place offerings of favorite foods for any loved ones who have died in the past year, in their memory. Spend some time visiting with them, remembering them. Listen for the Crone's voice in the rising Samhain wind. At midnight, bring out your Tarot cards and do the spreads of your choice to find out what the winter may bring.

Yule

Winter solstice, the longest night of the year, around December 22. Now the days will slowly begin to lengthen—this is a celebration of the sun's birth. Honor the return of hope. Choose the Inner Child Seven, Nine, or Ten of Crystals, or the Star.

This is a lovely time to give Tarot decks as gifts, if you know the preferences of the receiver. And if you feel that you have outgrown a deck, if it is no longer right for you, it will make a wonderful addition to your Yule fire: Tarot decks, unlike so many other things, are not recommended for recycling.

Continued play with Tarot is likely to take us on the same journey as the gradual progression in this book, from the personal to the universal. Recognition of the magick in Tarot images, and their gift of connecting the sacred and the everyday, gives us a deeply satisfying sense of oneness with the Deeper Powers, with all life on this planet, and with all aspects of the Self.

As Z. Budapest says in her *Holy Book of Women's Mysteries,* "There is no division between body and soul. One is not despised and the other glorified ... both come from the same source, the Mother. There is no division of the spiritual and profane, all is interrelated with everything else in the universe, and none stands apart from nature. All is Nature."

May we all come to know and celebrate our sacredness.

Blessed Be.

SUGGESTED READING

If you want more information on Tarot:

Almond, Jocelyn. *Tarot for Relationships.* San Francisco: Thorsons, 1990.

Arrien, Angeles. *The Tarot Handbook: Practical Applications of Ancient Visual Symbols.* Sonoma, CA: Arcus, 1987.

Bridges, Carol. *The Medicine Woman Inner Guidebook: A Woman's Guide to Her Unique Powers.* Nashville, IN: Earth Nation, 1987.

Doane, Doris C., and King Keyes. *How to Read Tarot Cards.* San Francisco: Harper Collins, 1979.

Eakins, Pamela. *Tarot of the Spirit.* New York: Samuel Weiser, 1992.

Fairfield, Gail, and Patti Provo. *Inspiration Tarot: A Workbook for Understanding and Creating Your Own Tarot Deck.* New York: Samuel Weiser, 1991.

Gray, Eden. *A Complete Guide to the Tarot.* New York: Bantam, 1972.

———. *The Tarot Revealed: A Modern Guide to Reading the Tarot Cards,* rev. ed. New York: NAL-Dutton, 1988.

Greer, Mary K. *Tarot Constellations: Patterns of Personal Destiny.* San Bernardino, CA: Borgo Press, 1988.

———. *Tarot Mirrors: Reflections of Personal Meaning.* San Bernardino, CA: Borgo Press, 1988.

———. *Tarot for Yourself: A Workbook for Personal Transformation.* San Bernardino, CA: Borgo Press, 1984.

Jayanti, Amber. *Living the Tarot: Applying the Ancient Oracle to the Challenges of Modern Life.* San Bernardino, CA: Borgo Press, 1988.

Johnson, Cait, and Maura D. Shaw. *Tarot Games: 45 Playful Ways to Explore Tarot Cards Together: A New Vision for the Circle of Community.* San Francisco: HarperSanFrancisco, 1994.

Knight, Gareth. *Tarot and Magic: Images for Ritual and Pathworking.* Rochester, VT: Inner Tradition, 1991.

Morgan, Frederick. *The Tarot of Cornelius Agrippa.* Sand Lake, NY: Sagarin Press, 1971.

Nichols, Sallie. *Jung and Tarot: An Archetypal Journey.* New York: Samuel Weiser, 1984.

Noble, Vicki. *Motherpeace: A Way to the Goddess through Myth, Art and Tarot.* San Francisco: Harper and Row, 1983.

Noble, Vicki, and Jonathan Tenney. *The Motherpeace Tarot Playbook: Astrology and the Motherpeace Cards.* Berkeley: Wingbow Press, 1986.

Peach, Emily. *Tarot Workbook: Understanding and Using Tarot Symbolism.* New York: Sterling, 1985.

Pollack, Rachel. *The New Tarot: Modern Variations of Ancient Images.* Woodstock, NY: Overlook Press, 1992.

————. *Seventy-Eight Degrees of Wisdom: A Book of Tarot: An in-depth analysis of the symbolism and psychological resonances of the Tarot suit cards, including instructions on how to give readings. Parts 1 and 2.* London: Aquarian Press, 1983.

————. *Tarot Readings and Meditations: How the Tarot can help us answer specific questions, act as a tool for psychological analysis and tell us how to overcome problems.* London: Aquarian Press, 1986.

Stuart, Micheline. *The Tarot Path to Self-Development.* Boston: Shambhala, 1990.

Waite, Arthur E. *A Pictorial Key to the Tarot.* New York: Citadel Press, 1979.

Walker, Barbara G. *The Secrets of the Tarot: Origins, History, and Symbolism.* San Francisco: HarperSanFrancisco, 1984.

If you would like to learn more about the Goddess, women's spirituality, Wise Woman healing ways, dreams, herbs, gemstones, food, astrology, rituals, and more:

Achterberg, Jeanne, Barbara Dossey, and Leslie Kolkmeier. *Rituals of Healing: Using Imagery for Health and Wellness.* New York: Bantam, 1994.

Beck, Renee, and Sydney Barbara Metrick. *The Art of Ritual.* Berkeley: Celestial Arts, 1990.

Beyerl, Paul. *The Master Book of Herbalism.* Custer, WA: Phoenix, 1984.

Blair, Nancy. *Amulets of the Goddess: Oracles of Ancient Wisdom.* Oakland, CA: Wingbow Press, 1993.

Budapest, Z. *Grandmother Moon: Lunar Magic in Our Lives.* San Francisco: HarperSanFrancisco, 1991.

————. *The Goddess in the Office.* San Francisco: HarperSanFrancisco, 1993.

————. *The Grandmother of Time.* San Francisco: HarperSanFrancisco, 1989.

————. *The Holy Book of Women's Mysteries,* rev. ed. Vols. 1 and 2. Berkeley: Wingbow Press, 1986.

Cahill, Sedonia, and Joshua Halpern. *The Ceremonial Circle: Practice, Ritual, and Renewal for Personal and Community Healing.* San Francisco: HarperSanFrancisco, 1992.

Campanelli, Pauline. *Ancient Ways: Reclaiming Pagan Traditions.* St. Paul, MN: Llewellyn, 1991.

————. *The Wheel of the Year: Living the Magickal Life.* St. Paul, MN: Llewellyn, 1987.

Cunningham, Scott. *The Complete Book of Incense, Oils, and Brews.* St. Paul, MN: Llewellyn, 1992.

———. *Cunningham's Encyclopedia of Crystal, Gem, and Metal Magic.* St. Paul, MN: Llewellyn, 1988.

———. *Cunningham's Encylopedia of Magical Herbs.* St. Paul, MN: Llewellyn, 1985.

———. *Magical Herbalism.* St. Paul, MN: Llewellyn, 1983.

———. *The Magic in Food.* St. Paul, MN: Llewellyn, 1991.

Delaney, Gayle. *Living Your Dreams.* New York: Harper and Row, 1979.

Dixon, Jo, and James Dixon. *The Color Book: Rituals, Charms and Enchantments from Castle Rising.* Denver, CO: J & J Enterprises, 1978.

———. *The Witches' Jewels: A Traditional Witches' Treatise: The Nature of Stones and Other Gifts of Mother Nature.* Morgantown, WV: Magickal Days, 1989.

Dolfyn. Crystal Wisdom: *Spiritual Properties of Crystals and Gemstones.* Oakland, CA: Earthspirit, 1989.

Duerk, Judith. *Circle of Stones.* San Diego: LuraMedia, 1989.

Eisler, Riane. *The Chalice and the Blade: Our History, Our Future.* San Francisco: HarperSanFrancisco, 1986.

Eisler, Riane, and David Loye. *The Partnership Way: New Tools for Living and Learning, Healing Our Families, Our Communities, and Our World.* San Francisco: Harper San Francisco, 1990.

Estés, Clarissa Pinkola. *Women Who Run with the Wolves: Myths and Stories of the Wild Woman Archetype.* New York: Ballantine, 1992.

Francia, Luisa. *Dragontime: Magic and Mystery of Menstruation.* Woodstock, NY: Ash Tree, 1988.

Garfield, Patricia. *Creative Dreaming.* New York: Ballantine, 1976.

———. *Your Child's Dreams.* New York: Ballantine, 1984.

Gawain, Shakti. *Creative Visualization.* Mill Valley, CA: Whatever, 1978.

Kinscher, Jonni. *Dreams Can Help: A Journal Guide to Understanding Your Dreams and Making Them Work for You.* Minneapolis: Free Spirit, 1988.

Kofalk, Harriet. *The Peaceful Cook.* Eugene, OR: Talking Leaves, 1991.

Luxton, Leonora. *Astrology, Key to Self Understanding.* St. Paul, MN: Llewellyn, 1978.

Mariechild, Diane. *Mother Wit: A Guide to Healing and Psychic Development.* Freedom, CA: Crossing Press, 1988.

Martz, Sandra, ed. *When I Am an Old Woman I Shall Wear Purple.* Watsonville, CA: Papier-Mache Press, 1991.

McLeester, Dick. *Welcome to the Magic Theater: A Handbook for Exploring Dreams.* Amherst, MA: Food for Thought, 1977.

Monaghan, Patricia. *The Book of Goddesses and Heroines.* New York: E. P. Dutton, 1981.

Murphy, Joseph M. *Santeria: African Spirits in America*. Boston: Beacon Press, 1993.

Noble, Vicki. *Shakti Woman: Feeling Our Fire, Healing Our World: The New Female Shamanism*. New York: Harper Collins, 1991.

———. *Uncoiling the Snake: Ancient Patterns in Contemporary Women's Lives*. San Francisco: HarperSanFrancisco, 1993.

Robertson, Laurel, Carol Flinders, and Brian Ruppenthal. *The New Laurel's Kitchen: A Handbook for Vegetarian Cookery and Nutrition*. Berkeley: Ten Speed Press, 1986.

Sakoian, Frances, and Louis S. Acker. *The Astrologer's Handbook*. New York: Harper and Row, 1973.

Starck, Marcia. *Earth Mother Astrology: Ancient Healing Wisdom*. St. Paul, MN: Llewellyn, 1989.

———. *Women's Medicine Ways: Cross-Cultural Rites of Passage*. Freedom, CA: Crossing Press, 1993.

Starhawk. *Dreaming the Dark: Magic, Sex, and Politics*. Boston: Beacon Press, 1982.

———. *The Spiral Dance: A Rebirth of the Ancient Religion of the Great Goddess: Rituals, Invocations, Exercises, Magic*. San Francisco: Harper and Row, 1989.

———. *Truth or Dare*. San Francisco: Harper Collins, 1989.

Stein, Diane. *All Women Are Healers: A Comprehensive Guide to Natural Healing*. Freedom, CA: Crossing Press, 1990.

———. *The Women's Spirituality Book*. St. Paul, MN: Llewellyn, 1987.

Stone, Merlin. *Ancient Mirrors of Womanhood: Our Goddess and Heroine Heritage*. New York: New Sibylline, 1979.

———. *When God Was a Woman*. New York: Harcourt Brace Jovanovich, 1978.

Teish, Luisa. *Jambalaya: The Natural Woman's Book of Personal Charms and Practical Rituals*. San Francisco: Harper and Row, 1985.

Walker, Barbara G. *The Crone*. San Francisco: Harper and Row, 1985.

———. *Women's Rituals*. San Francisco: Harper and Row, 1990.

Weed, Susun. *Healing Wise*. Woodstock, NY: Ash Tree, 1989.

———. *Wise Woman Ways for the Menopausal Years*. Woodstock, NY: Ash Tree, 1992.

Weinstein, Marion. *Earth Magic: A Dianic Book of Shadows*. Custer, WA: Phoenix, 1986.

———. *Positive Magic: Occult Self-Help*. Custer, WA: Phoenix, 1984.

Worth, Valerie. *The Crone's Book of Words*. St. Paul, MN: Llewellyn, 1986.

ACKNOWLEDGMENTS

I offer my deepest thanks to Maura D. Shaw, coauthor, editor, dear friend, and now publisher, whose support for my work has had such a profound and marvelous effect on my life and whose brilliance, incredibly diverse talents, and personal charm are a continual inspiration. I am eternally grateful that the Goddess brought us together. And my appreciative thanks to Joe Tantillo for his delicious illustrations and for being such a gentle delight to work with. An author just couldn't ask for a more nourishing and insightful publishing team.

I also owe a great debt to the many teachers, authors, and Wise Ones whose work is the foundation of my own, especially Z. Budapest, Vicki Noble, Starhawk, and Susun Weed. And I am forever grateful to Jessie Christiansen, who first introduced me to the Goddess, and who was such a wise mentor and guide; Nadine Daugherty, whose sister-presence is always at the heart of any work I do; Elaine Fletcher, Hestia Irons, and Regina Siegel for all of their nurturing, healing, and support; Raven Wild, who first taught me about the miraculous health-giving weeds growing in my yard and opened my eyes to the Wise Woman way; and the women with whom I have danced in Circle. Blessed be to all of you. You always remind me that we are Goddess.

To my parents—Pat Johnson, who first taught me how to live everyday life with artistry and grace, and Bob Johnson, with his love of the playful and of the green growing things— my loving thanks for giving me the seeds of this book.

And my gratitude always to Stu Hannan, patient partner and chief support, and to Reid, our son, who circles through my life and work like an irresistible whirlwind of tenderness and creativity.

About the Author

Cait Johnson is a writer, artist, and Tarot teacher who has been actively involved in the reclamation of Goddess-centered spirituality for many years, teaching workshops on the cards, dreamwork, and ritual-making, and facilitating Full Moon circles for women. Her first book, *Tarot Games: 45 Playful Ways to Explore Tarot Cards Together: A New Vision for the Circle of Community,* coauthored with Maura D. Shaw, is currently available from HarperSanFrancisco. She lives near the Hudson River with her partner, their son, and three cats.